F**K PLAN B

How to scale your technology
business faster and achieve Plan A.

DOMINIC MONKHOUSE

Praise for Dominic Monkhouse and 'F**k Plan B'

Understanding how to find our A-players, keeping those we want to grow and losing those too toxic to stay has been a real challenge, yet game changer for us at Excelsior.

It was through Dominic introducing high-quality tools validated through his own strategic practice in business which has made all this possible, actually happen and making such a difference.
- Hazel Pulley, CEO Excelsior MAT -

Working with Dominic has caused us to become much more focused on working on the business rather than in the business. However, it is no walk in the park and requires an unrelenting pursuit of continuous improvement and being held to account. We have begun to see a direct impact on the business as a result of the rhythms that he has taught us to implement. His style is a coaching one and is deeply relational with his support. Dominic has a wealth of knowledge which seems to tumble out in fluid conversations, enhancing the experience even more and to such an extent that I have learnt the diligence to quickly take notes so as to not miss the moment of added learning.
- Tom Frame, Group MD Etch and BigRadical -

Dominic has experience in many areas that almost any question you ask he has a great story or insight which helps solve the challenge!
- Daniel Teacher, Managing Director T-Tech -

Working with Dominic has highlighted that no matter how much prior experience you have, or think you have, you always need an independent sounding board and someone that challenges you.

What has surprised me in working with Dominic, is that in many cases seemingly small changes and pieces of advice can make a massive impact on performance.

Relentless focus on the priorities that drive plan A, and the positive energy that this creates, mean you dont waste time worrying about Plan B!!
- David Howson, CEO Six Degrees -

Dominic has been an incredible support to both me and my team since we started working together.

Dominic has helped us develop real clarity of what we need to be doing as a business in order to achieve the success we desire. He's coupled this with also helping us construct a clear strategy of how to achieve our goals whilst enabling us to identify opportunities to the market to place the brand and how to communicate and promote it.

Put Simply, Dominic is just brilliant at business. I am so grateful to be able to access his mind and garner his advice. I feel a real strength in knowing that he is by our side.
- Cate Murden, CEO PUSH -

My understanding is that the vast majority of business owners never studied business at school or university. Many owners either fall into ownership or are great innovators who spot an opportunity, which subsequently takes off with a mixture of luck, demand and after few good decisions turns into a business. I keep hearing `The first £100,000" is the hardest £100K, to be honest, every new £100K step is really difficult, especially when the only money you have is your own and that is limited. Over the past 20 years of running Clearvision, I can reflect back and see considerable changes in myself. Self-reflection has been an important part of my journey and without any shadow of a doubt, it is easier done when you have a coach you can confide in and 100% trust. I have been lucky to have two excellent coaches in my time Ian Prince and Dom Monkhouse.

Whilst I do not have any regrets in my business life there are two stand out things which I would change and thus encourage other business owners to do. The first is to carve out time to read business books. For many years I believed I did not have time to read business books. I believed running the business was where all my time and energy should be spent. The reality is there are many excellent books which will save you time. The second is to find a coach or mentor or be part of a network of CEO's who can share life experiences. Most good coaches operate within a framework, for me and Clearvision, the Ideal framework was ScalingUp and 3HAG.
- Gerry Tombs, CEO Clearvision -

ABOUT THE AUTHOR

---- * ----

Dominic Monkhouse
The UK's premium technology industry business coach

Dominic Monkhouse is the CEO and Founder of Monkhouse & Company, a no-bullsh*t coaching company that helps the best CEOs reach their goals faster.

In the last two recessions (9/11 and GFC) Dominic has scaled two UK technology service firms to £30m within five years. He learned which execution systems worked, made plenty of mistakes, tried, tested and discarded other tools and discovered innovative strategies that disrupted competitors. At Rackspace, they grew to 150 people on the team at £30m. At Peer 1 Hosting the team was 120 in the UK at £30m. The team went on to grow Peer 1 Hosting globally from Can$94m to $200m before exiting for $650m.

Over the past 6 years, Dominic has empowered many CEOs and their leadership teams. He has now created a purpose-built Management Lab on his farm in Wiltshire, where he shares the systems, tools and strategies that enabled him to scale.

Billed as "the happy entrepreneur", Dominic has been called "Britain's Best Boss", cited in the Daily Telegraph as the creator of the "best office in Britain" and has been welcomed on the BBC Breakfast show to talk about his work.

ARE YOU READY FOR RAPID, SIGNIFICANT AND SUSTAINABLE GROWTH?

Visit scale up expert Dominic Monkhouse at
www.monkhouseandcompany.com,
or come join his Management Lab in Wiltshire.
For enquiries please call 01725 605900 or
email dom@monkhouseandcompany.com.

*Only those who will risk going too far
can possibly find out how far one can go*
- T.S. Eliot

TABLE OF CONTENTS

———— * ————

INTRODUCTION

———— * ————

Scaling up a business is one of the hardest things you can do. But it is one of the most rewarding. A scale up is defined as *having achieved growth in revenue or headcount of 20% year over year for three years.* It's not easy to grow consistently or sustainably year on year, but it is possible - and I've done it. In fact, I have a track record of scaling up a series of award-winning technology businesses, growing them from zero revenue to £30 million within five years.

Scaling up is hard work. No matter what sector you are in, you're going to need energy, drive and fanatical attention to detail. You also need to train yourself to have a perpetually inquisitive outlook that thrives on learning new things and absorbing the latest thinking.

Scaling up your operation constitutes a sea change in management thinking, a shift in perspective and a skill set that many entrepreneurs have yet to master. So often, I meet people who want to expand their businesses but don't have this growth mindset. They're not reading 12 or more books a year. Or going to conferences. Or prioritising training and development in their businesses. They are not taking action. If this is you, this book is going to be an eye-opener. You will either be exposed to a whole new way of thinking, and embrace the change that will lead to success, or you will at least understand where you are going wrong (and it is then your choice if you want to rest on your laurels or take action to create the conditions needed to succeed).

It's important to acknowledge that the following chapters focus mainly on culture. That's because it was cultural changes that made the biggest difference to our growth at Rackspace and Peer 1. This is not a book about strategy. But if there's a fire in your belly and a real desire to put a dent in the universe, keep reading and take notes. I've been there and know what it takes to scale a technology business through a recession. Let's make sure we're clear on the prize. You're aiming to:

a) reduce the time it takes for your senior team to manage the operational activities of your business by 80%,

b) allow them to focus outward on market-facing activities,

c) realign team members to drive execution and results.

According to Verne Harnish, founder of EO and author of 'Scaling Up: How a Few Companies Make It...and Why the Rest Don't, (Rockefeller Habits 2.0)', firms who succeed at scaling up have double the rate of cash flow, triple the industry average for profitability and an increased valuation relative to competitors. And, best of all, the stakeholders (owners, shareholders, employees and customers) enjoy the journey.

PART 1

WHERE ARE YOU NOW?
WHAT'S HOLDING YOU BACK?

WHERE ARE YOU NOW?

———— * ————

Before you set random targets and start blindly throwing darts trying to hit them, it's important to start with a comprehensive understanding of where your business is right now, and what its purpose is.

It's so important to take a step back and bring a laser-focus into your business. Invest time and energy now to find a clearer direction and it will pay you back in spades. Your company is much more likely to achieve the growth it's capable of if you know the direction it's going and what's holding it back.

People yearn for certainty and meaning within their lives, and businesses do too. Your team members want to know what they are working towards, the customers need to believe in what they are buying, and the managers need a North Star to guide them. This can become an anchor in the turbulent waters of world events. This is the essence of finding the core purpose of your business.

Businesses with a genuine sense of purpose tend to be more successful.

Defining your company's core purpose is likely to be the most important strategic decision you'll ever make. Yet most people exist in businesses with no purpose. They go through the motions every day – turn up to work, do an okay job, and go home again. No loyalty, no engagement, no joy. I can't help thinking about a poster I saw in one of my first jobs at Marks and Spencer: *'Doing a good job around here is like pissing yourself in a dark suit. You'll get a warm feeling but no-one else will notice'.* What a dismal way for your team members and yourself to think about work.

But before you consider how your team members feel you first need to get super-clear on your purpose. Go ahead, write down the purpose of your business now:

....

....

....

....

If you were able to write down the purpose easily, congratulations, you can move onto the next step. If not, here is your first thinking point.

Look to your marketing materials and your taglines, what do they say you do? These are all clues to how your business shows up every day. What is the problem you are fixing in the world? What is the reason for this firm's existence? What is its purpose?

WILL YOU GET ANYWHERE IF YOU DON'T KNOW WHERE YOU'RE HEADING?

Once you've worked out your purpose, you can use it to bring focus to everything that you do. Many of my clients also have a 'BHAG®' (a Big Hairy Audacious Goal), a term coined by management thinker Jim Collins in his 2005 book *Built To Last: Successful Habits of Visionary Companies*. A BHAG is a 10 to 30-year target to aim for, something inspiring that creates a sense of urgency and excitement in your company.

Your company is more likely to succeed if you can identify the one thing you do best.

This sounds simple but it will take time to define, working through three specific areas:

Firstly, isolate the things that give your company energy and passion. Look at what gets you and your team out of bed early in the morning and keeps you working late voluntarily.

Secondly, define the one thing that you can be best in the world at – something you know you can do better than anyone else. You'll reach this conclusion by recognising what you'll never be best at. Be honest and don't shy away from this. It's all part of working out your true strengths.

Finally, examine the things that drive your economic engine in terms of profitability and market potential.

The intersection of these three ideas is your BHAG. This should act as your North Star, providing a constant direction to steer your company forwards. It may mean letting go of some things you do and attaching more tightly to others. You may need to learn to say 'No' more often than you're used to. You will definitely have to address some roadblocks holding you back.

I will address the core principles needed to create a successful business in Part 2 of this book, but you must first find your *why* (purpose) and your *what* (BHAG). This is what I work on first with my clients, and simply by aligning your business to its purpose and BHAG can you put in motion growth, revenue and excellence.

WHAT'S HOLDING YOU BACK?

———— ✳ ————

While lacking a clearly defined purpose and BHAG can hold tech-orientated businesses back, I've also identified a set of common roadblocks that you'll need to smash through in order to achieve the growth you crave. These are easier to identify and combat than finding your overall purpose, but they need a strong sense of leadership and teamwork to overcome them.

1. LOSS OF MOMENTUM

It's common for start-ups to plateau at a certain size. They start with clear visions, limitless energy and an abundance of ideas, but over time these get lost and lose their momentum. The culture has fallen away and the thing that originally drove the company forward has stalled. When an organisation is small, the founders need to live and breathe the culture so team members will follow their lead. By the time it reaches a team of 100, the influence of the founders starts to wane. They are less involved in recruitment so may not have personally hired everyone. There's now a distance between the founders' view of where the company is heading and the organisation's direction. What shows up as part of this loss of momentum is that things take longer to get done, decision making becomes painful and team members start second-guessing each other.

ential to nail down your purpose, core values and BHAG the very beginning and then introduce a process where they discussed and reviewed regularly. My advice is to check in on this every quarter and review for fit annually. This will bring clarity and consistency to your business, making it possible to make fast decisions again. As you grow, customers will ask for things that don't fit with the purpose of your company and it's easy to fall into a cash/execution revenue trap. Use your BHAG as a North Star, guiding you towards the right decisions. Say 'no' more often than you say 'yes'. Default to no.

2. RECRUITING THE WRONG PEOPLE

As CEO of a business that's scaling up, you need to get hands-on with the first 50 people that you hire. It's vitally important that you get this right. These people are the white cells in your business – its immune system – and form the basis of your tribe. My advice is to hire slow and fire fast. Make sure your first 50 team members are rock solid on your core behaviours and values because this will give you the foundation you need for sustainable, consistent growth.

Achieving true clarity over your BHAG and purpose should automatically boost your brand. What journey are you on? Is it an interesting enough mission to attract the 'A Players' you need to succeed? People tend to think in linear terms when it comes to talent. They expect their best people to be twice as good as average. But in fact, the difference is often exponential. So, for the same job in the same location, you can get a person 10x or 100x better than the average.

These 'A Players' don't necessarily need more money. According to Dan Pink, in his book *Drive: The Surprising Truth About What Motivates Us,* they're looking for a workplace that gives them autonomy, mastery and purpose. If you can create an environment that fosters these things, you'll attract great people and they will be far more productive and profitable.

Once you've got this solid base, you need to create a hiring system that ensures A Players continue to be recruited. Apply a sales mentality to this process. Ensure every aspect of the candidate experience is managed. Be obsessive. When I was MD of Peer 1 in Southampton, I decided that hiring decisions should be made by someone who hadn't met the candidate. The hiring manager would take into consideration the Gallup Strength Assessment, the CV, interview notes and a picture the candidate had drawn, off the cuff, to represent what motivated and inspired them. The decision was made based on whether this person would fit with our purpose, core values and make a cultural contribution. Don't hire people who aren't going to make a difference, rather take a decision to raise the average within the firm.

Try not to make the mistake of going cheap on salary. It's fine to recruit less experienced people and grow them because they have the potential to be amazing. But hiring people who should already be amazing because of their age or experience – but aren't – is a death knell. You may perceive them to be cheap, but it will cost you far more in the long run. It's guaranteed to p*ss off your existing A Players – I see this costly mistake happening all the time in businesses I work with.

As part of your regular talent review, it is vital to identify the rock stars who live and breathe your organisation and embodying the values you want to encourage in others. Make sure you call them out for this, setting them up as role models and giving them recognition and praise. This will give other team members something to aspire to and is a great way to embed the culture you need to grow.

If people aren't the right fit, be ruthless. I suggest asking your managers to review their team on a monthly basis. Would they enthusiastically rehire all of them tomorrow? If not, they need to go. Put a mechanism in place so that it's not only management's job to spot poor performance. Wherever I've been MD, I've made it a priority to take old hands out for lunch. I knew they had a useful 'spider-sense'. They could tell instinctively whether a new team member was genuinely a 'Racker' or 'Peer' or 'Labber' ie. a member of our tribe.

Finally, make sure there's no place in your organisation for brilliant jerks. If the behaviours don't fit, even if the performance does, they need to take their toxic ways somewhere else.

3. POOR DECISIONS ON STRUCTURE

Professor Robin Dunbar from Oxford University suggested that *'the human mind is only capable of handling around 150 relationships simultaneously'*. As companies get bigger than 150 people, it's impossible to know everyone individually or understand where they sit in relationship to each other. I'm intrigued by this.

As companies grow, there comes a point when team members stop putting their cups in the dishwasher and there's less shared ownership for general issues like fixing broken equipment and keeping the office tidy. This often coincides with the introduction of new, hierarchical structures which create silos and more opportunities for a 'them and us' attitude to creep in. You've gone from a smaller team of generalists where everyone wears multiple hats and knows what's going on, to a functional, departmental structure. And this starts to impact on customer satisfaction.

Sometimes, new team members bring bureaucracy with them. It's often the result of hiring senior people from large corporates who have big company habits. Presented with a challenge, they'll try to introduce a whole new set of rules and structure. Beware! This can kill productivity in A Players. All they need to excel is freedom and a framework of organisational expectations. They certainly do not need bureaucracy around expenses, holidays, salaries or, the horror of horrors, annual appraisals!

Try to avoid the trap of thinking that a functional, departmental structure is necessary. I'm a big fan of small, multi-functional teams and this is the structure I have always implemented.

It's fine to have some shared support services but try and put as much as possible into the team. By focusing teams on a small number of customers, you'll have much higher levels of engagement. Their work will feel more purposeful and fulfilling. And there's a much higher chance of that team delivering great service compared to if they were split into functions.

A final word on structure – working hard is not the same as getting good outcomes. As you get bigger, you need to get less worried about hours and more focused on objectives and key results (OKRs). Some people may appear to be working hard but they're actually delivering nothing. You need to put in a structure that ensures expectations are understood. Your team needs to know what a good day looks like. As my companies scaled, we introduced strong indicators – the number of tickets dealt with, a Net Promoter Score (NPS) by engineer, meaningful customer conversations on the phone, recurring revenue achieved per month etc. This made it much easier to have the occasional, but necessary, difficult conversation with the team.

4. FAILURE OF COMMUNICATION

As your company grows, the rapid intensity of change can cause resistance and, before you know it, negativity can creep in like a disease at the heart of your business. The solution is always communication. But, as life gets busier, no-one seems to have the time for it. So, when it's needed most, it's neglected.

In the beginning, it's not a big deal. When you're part of a small team on a mission to change the world, communication comes easily. The bigger you get, the more important it becomes, particularly if you have multiple sites. My advice is to introduce a communication rhythm as early as you can. Daily, weekly, monthly, quarterly, annually – you need regular opportunities for bottom-up and top-down comms.

This will maintain momentum like nothing else, ensuring objectives and key results are always fully understood. Progress on your various themes can be discussed as well as customer success stories. You'll also have the opportunity to dish out social currency, reinforcing the right behaviours by telling good news stories about people who've done well. Praise and celebration are so important to employee engagement.

5. LOSS OF CUSTOMER FOCUS

When I see companies that are stalling, unable to articulate their strategy and unsure of where to go next, it's often because they don't spend enough time talking to their customers. Executive teams get busy in their individual silos and leave customer relationships to Sales or Customer Service.

Why is this bad? Well, it comes back to your purpose. Why is your company here? It's because you spotted that a group of customers have a problem that you're trying to fix. Proximity to this is vital. Otherwise, you might end up spending time and effort fixing a problem you think they have, only to find out later that this is wrong. You need your company to be customer-centric.

If you're looking to scale up, every member of your leadership team should be committed to speaking with a customer every week. The attribution mapping can be really useful here because it forces your team to step back and look at your market in relation to your competitors. By truly understanding the competitive attributes of your company and market you'll be able to develop a unique strategy that will give you forward momentum for growth.

The 5 roadblocks (and how to overcome them):

1. **Loss of momentum** - overcome by setting a clear purpose, set of values and BHAG. Review it quarterly, and check for fit annually. Your BHAG should be your North Star.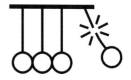

2. **Recruiting the wrong people** - you need to hire the first 50 members of your team. They need to carry your core values and behaviours forward. Pay for genuine talent, and give your A players a chance to shine. If they don't fit, fire fast.

3. **Poor decisions on structure** - avoid the functional, departmental structure. Try to keep a small, agile and multi-functional structure. Give your team members freedom and a framework for excellence.

4. **Failure of communication** - create a communication rhythm, daily, weekly and quarterly. Discuss success stories, key objectives reached and praise good team members. Get the senior leadership team to speak to people not in their teams.

5. **Loss of customer focus** - leadership's proximity to the customer is vital. They need to be talking to customers too. You need your company to be customer-centric.

Scaling-up is a tough road – there's no getting away from it. It's easy to lose your sense of direction, hitting one roadblock after another. It's important to address where your business is now, in order to move onto the next steps. In part 2 and part 3 of this book, I will discuss the core principles of business success and give you a 10 point plan for scaling your business. But before you keep reading, take some time to understand where your business is now and what roadblocks are present. Don't worry, with conviction, drive and determination, it's possible to smash through to the other side. When you do, the rewards will be worth it. And it will be fun.

PART 2

THE 5 CORE PRINCIPLES OF BUSINESS SUCCESS

After reviewing Part 1 of this book and taking stock of where you are as a company, and what potential roadblocks you face, you are ready to move onto the next stage in the scale up process.

Perhaps you have amassed a talented team of people with energy and determination. Your vision is clear and you have set a strong BHAG that everyone in the business aligns with. Your business model has achieved product market fit and now you're ready for the challenges of scaling-up. You are a CEO on a mission and you are raring to grow!

I've been there. In my career as Managing Director for two fast-growing tech companies, I've faced the roadblocks and challenges, and smashed through them to create rapid, significant and sustainable growth. And what I've learned is that there are 5 core principles that are at the heart of any successful scale up.

1. MAKING YOUR CUSTOMER KING WITH A NET PROMOTER SCORE®

Many companies say they put the customer first, but the reality is often different. I know so many organisations that work to minimum standards laid down by Service Level Agreements (SLAs). As MD of Rackspace, it was obvious to me that our competitors used their SLAs to define the worst experience a customer could expect and this was often what they got. If the SLA said a ticket would be answered in 15 minutes, the customer got a response at 14 minutes and 59 seconds. Because these organisations saw service as a cost, there was a denial of service mentality. Don't fall into this trap.

We decided to do things differently at Rackspace. Our purpose was 'Fanatical Support®' and this became our internal and external benchmark. We did have SLAs but we changed our mindset around them. If we breached them, we paid out. What we did and what was in the contract were two different things. Instead of waiting for the customer to notice they'd had an outage, we proactively rang them to offer a credit. They were blown away by this. We'd find that a service failure would often lead to more business from our customers through higher levels of trust gained from our honest approach. This enabled us to achieve class-leading NPS (Net Promoter Score) numbers in the high 70s or low 80s.

Net Promoter Score first came to my attention, with Fred Reichheld's 2003 article in the Harvard Business Review (HBR) 'The One Number You Need to Grow'. If you are looking to implement NPS yourself read Reichheld's *'The Ultimate Question 2.0: How Net Promoter Companies Thrive in a Customer-Driven World'.*

It's a leap of faith to believe that delivering better customer service than your competitors will make you more successful financially. It's not something you can necessarily prove on a spreadsheet. Most businesses tend to measure and manage the cost side of the business but don't have a metric for measuring customer satisfaction or engagement. I was lucky that I turned up at Rackspace at a point where I could see how it played out. In 2001, we were selling single servers at £99 per month. Five years later, we had a £30m turnover in the UK and some of our customers were spending around £50,000 a month. This transformation came about because we were genuinely customer obsessed.

Our customer-first mentality impacted our recruitment hugely. Our competitors were stuck in a 'denial of service' mindset meaning new recruits from our industry came with all the baggage and behaviours that we didn't want. So, we looked at other customer-focused sectors. Some of our best people came from hospitality – we hired waitresses, bar-employees, door-people. And loads of South Africans. Their customer hero skills were spot on. They would throw themselves on an unexploded bomb for a customer. In fact, they'd go looking for that unexploded bomb! Doing a good job for their customers gave them real satisfaction and personal joy.

I've rolled out NPS as a metric to measure customer satisfaction in all three of the businesses where I was MD. To really improve our score, we told every director that they must speak to at least one customer every week. As a result, in every meeting, we had first-hand feedback from around 10 customers and when we made a decision, we knew it was intimately connected to our customers.

'WOULD YOU RECOMMEND [NAME OF COMPANY] TO A FRIEND OR COLLEAGUE?'

It's always puzzled me why so many businesses focus on finding new customers rather than keeping the ones they've got? Research from the Harvard Business Review shows that it costs five times more to do this. And this is even more crazy as existing customers are 50% more likely to try new products compared to new customers. Increasing customer retention rates by 5% increases profits by anything between 25 and 95%. That's staggering growth.

But making your customers your cheerleaders doesn't happen overnight. It takes a deliberate strategy, time, and a metric to score their happiness – the Net Promoter Score. So, what were the reasons I chose this metric? Why is NPS so effective to growing businesses?

THE NET PROMOTER SCORE

In a world where customer surveys can be endless, NPS is a real breath of fresh air. Back in the day, I worked with complicated customer satisfaction surveys with 50 questions, giving me an end score of 4.93. What the hell did that mean? No-one knew! So I started to look for a better metric.

Fred Reichheld spent two years refining a single, all-important question. It needed to link the survey responses with actual customer behaviour (purchasing patterns and referrals) and ultimately with company growth. He tested a number of forms of words and eventually landed on, *'Would you recommend (name of company) to a friend or colleague?'* The answer to this question is given on a scale of 0-10. If customers give you a 9 or 10, they are a 'promoter', a 7 or 8 they are 'passive' and 0 – 6 a 'detractor'. Subtracting the percentage of detractors from the percentage of promoters gives a Net Promoter Score of anything between -100 to +100.

"How likely is it that you would recommend [company X] to a friend or colleague?" Ten means "extremely likely" to recommend, five means neutral, and zero means "not at all likely." When we examined customer referral and repurchase behaviors along this scale, we found three logical clusters. "Promoters," the customers with the highest rates of repurchase and referral, gave ratings of nine or ten to the question. The "passively satisfied" logged a seven or an eight, and "detractors" scored from zero to six.

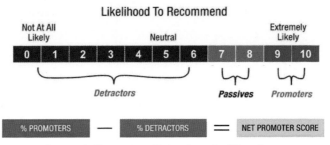

Image 1: Promoters, Detractors And Passives
Source: The Ultimate Question 2.0 Fred Reichheld

What has always struck me is 9 or 10 is a high bar. In previous customer satisfaction exercises, companies would have been delirious with a score of 7 or 8! In fact, they would probably have counted anyone giving a score of 5 or more as satisfied. What NPS is saying is that customers that give you 5s and 6s hate you, 7s and 8s don't really care and only 9s or 10s are worth your additional effort as they are the ones that will spend more and refer you.

Other customer satisfaction surveys seem to be more about patting yourself on the back and saying, 'We're not sh*t'. But they don't tell you whether a customer will churn. These traditional surveys may give you superficially good satisfaction scores, but you'll still find customers leaving or buying stuff from your competitors. NPS tells you that, unless they're super engaged, you haven't got them anywhere.

Business is all about relationships you've built with your customers. When you use NPS, as well as scoring you, your customers are asked to tell you why they've given you that score. I've always taken these free text comments and rung clients up afterwards – they're a heaven sent opportunity to build a relationship. This makes your clients feel heard – a rare thing in surveys. Perhaps you can offer them a credit or discuss what you could have done differently. You can use NPS as an on-going mechanism to build relationships.

NPS is a behavioural metric. It accurately measures the degree to which your customers are emotionally connected to you. This is important because the more connected they are, the more they are likely to cut you some slack in times of difficulty. If you have a service failure, you'll have in-built resilience.

At Rackspace, NPS became our secret weapon. We grew 1% every month, even if we didn't win new customers. Across the IT industry, our competitors were either flat or shrinking if they didn't pull in more customers at the top. Paying attention to the 'leaky bucket' drove profitability through our purpose of 'Fanatical Support'.

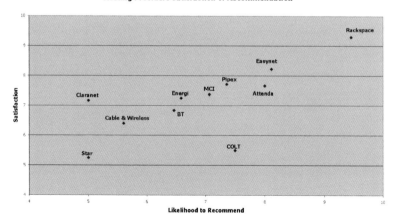

Image 2: Rackspace Likelihood To Recommend
Source: Vanson Bourne Research 2005

Most other IT companies saw service as a cost and were in a cost/service minimisation mindset. We were completely the opposite. We were mad on service! Totally unlimited. It was all about maximising NPS and through doing that, everything else would take care of itself – and it did. Spectacularly!

WHEN TO USE NPS

Traditionally, satisfaction exercises are done annually, on the same day, for all clients. With NPS you have flexibility. You can break the surveys down into manageable chunks and do some elements of your customer base over time. In the past, we've decided on a certain number of clients every week to get a 3-month rolling average. This is far less overwhelming, giving the opportunity to digest daily, weekly and monthly data that can feed into course corrections or changes to products, service or people. It's all about getting into a regular rhythm.

Put in place NPS and you'll have an efficient early warning system to alert you to any issues with customers before they do too much damage. Instead of waiting for an annual customer survey, you can sort things out fast. You'll quickly identify unhappy clients who've had a service failure and you can get in there quickly with remediation. Research shows that if you can spot and fix problems, your customers will love you more than if there was no service failure in the first place. Read 'Moments of Truth' by former Scandanavian Airlines president Jan Carlzon for a great case study on how to get your customers to love you.

Generally, you'll find the customers who are motivated enough to fill in the NPS surveys want you to do better. It's the ones who don't bother that you should be really worried about. They're not even engaged enough to tell you you've been sh*t! You need to find out if you're asking the right people. Have you uncovered an expectation gap? Are they the wrong customer for you? Is there a mismatch somewhere?

NPS will help you spot where 90% of your future profit is going to come from. Imagine the power of this information! You can slice the data, focusing on specific customer cohorts. You want all your most profitable customers to be giving you 9s or 10s so the focus should be on keeping these people happy specifically. At Peer 1, our top 5% of customers were worth 60% of our revenue. You can guess who got the most attention! We restructured several times to focus more resources on improving the service delivery to this cohort.

Don't assume it's going to be your biggest clients that are your most profitable. Some smaller customers may be great advocates of your brand with the power to refer you to others who become big spenders. Pay attention to that small digital agency – they might refer you to every one of their clients! A good book to read on this is 'The Value Profit Chain' by Heskett, Sasser and Schlesinger. They discuss the relationships of loyalty, trust and satisfaction with customers and other stakeholders.

If you're using NPS effectively, all of your quarterly targets should contain some reference to NPS data. Customer cohorts can be created to prioritise fixes. So, for the next quarter, ask yourself, 'What is the big thing that we're going to fix that will drive an uptick in our NPS over time?'

You may find cohorts of customers that are less important to the organisation. If the NPS is not so high in these areas, you can decide that you won't focus any additional effort here. Tell your team and explain this to the customers. Accept that you might lose them or even may have to fire them. You can't do everything. Keep your eye on the bigger prize.

NPS CHANGES CULTURE AND MINDSET

One of the best things about NPS for me is its ability to shift mindset and culture in a business. On a philosophical level, it creates a culture of seeking criticism. If you're constantly told you're amazing, you're not likely to change anything. But if you have a mechanism where you're receiving a lower score than a 9, you can ask 'What could we have done better?' This is what happened at Rackspace. Our culture sought criticism so it could improve.

NPS will tell you the truth about your organisation. And if you're uncomfortable with that, then it's better to not do it at all as you'll set false expectations in your customers and employees. But if you are serious about scaling up, growing your business and creating value for your customers, then NPS is an essential tool to connect with your customers.

2. COMMUNICATION

Change is inevitable in a growing business. But have you considered that some team members might struggle with it?

Humans are creatures of habit and we prefer to stick with what we know. This can cause problems when you're scaling your business. The rapid intensity of change often causes resistance, and negativity can creep in like a disease at the heart of your business. The solution? Communicate. Communicate. And communicate some more!

The irony is that as a business goes through rapid growth, no-one seems to have the time for communication. So, when it's needed most, it's neglected. To get under the skin of a new client, I'll turn up at their offices and chat to their team. When I ask them, 'How's the business doing?' they'll often reply, 'No idea. They never tell me.' I probe further and they tell me, 'There were some big announcements a while back but I haven't heard anything since'. It's common for team members to feel their company has loads of great ideas but doesn't seem to finish any of them.

Sound familiar? The good news is, it's simple to fix. As with anything worth doing, it takes deliberate practice and focus before it becomes ingrained. So how do you ensure your communication rhythm is in sync with your business growth?

SET A RHYTHM AND MANAGE EXPECTATIONS

We've all been there. Sitting in a crowded airport, surrounded by screaming children, two of whom are yours. Your frustration builds as time passes without any indication of why your flight's delayed. A simple communication could make all the difference – even if it's to tell you there will be another announcement in 20 minutes' time. Constant communication keeps stress levels down. No communication creates uncertainty. People need to know what's happening and their expectations need to be managed.

Disappointment is often the result of incorrect expectation. I encourage my clients to say what they're not going to do as well as what they are. If you've recognised there's a problem, but it's less pressing than something bigger, at least tell people you've noticed and give them an indication of priority. This goes for customers as well as team members. If you've built a sense of forward momentum, you'll find that people will start to trust that their issue will get fixed eventually.

Rhythm is everything with communication. Daily, weekly, monthly and quarterly – you need regular opportunities for bottom up and top down comms. Daily huddles are a great way to encourage dialogue between team members and their managers, discussing team goals and everyday progress. I also suggest weekly one-on-ones with managers as well as monthly all-hands meetings, where the whole company gathers. These grease the wheels of a business, encouraging the sharing of information and ensuring everyone knows what's going on. It's impossible to have too much communication!

There are many tools out there that help to embed a regular comms rhythm. My current favourite is FridayPulse.com. It's a tool that gets everyone into a regular rhythm of giving feedback on a Friday and then meeting to discuss this on a Monday. This provides regular opportunities to share annoyances or celebrate someone's hard work. Really valuable stuff!

And if you have unhelpful communication rhythms? Then ditch them. Particularly annual appraisals – my pet hate! I don't think annual rhythms work. A quarterly cycle is much more effective, both in terms of performance development and goal setting. You can tell team members where they're going and what point they've reached on the journey. An annual horizon is too far away. Who can remember what they've done across a whole year? What's the point of telling someone that they've under-achieved for 12 months? This is a massive waste of precious time that could have been spent on fixing the issue. Daily feedback from managers is much more effective.

BOTTOM-UP COMMUNICATION

Many of my clients struggle to get feedback from their team. To them, communication feels like one-way traffic – too much top-down from the executive team and not enough from people on the front-line.

I was recently invited to observe an all-hands meeting and, afterwards, discussed how it had gone with the client. He was frustrated that no-one had asked any questions. 'I asked for feedback', he said, 'But they didn't come up with anything.' My observation was he hadn't waited long enough. There'd been an awkward silence that he was too quick to fill. Perhaps he needed to be more deliberate about seeking feedback? In future, all his team members should be told to prepare questions in advance. Then he could randomly select people if no one volunteered. He needed to make it really clear that this was his intention and, like any muscle, the organisation needed to work at it before it became second nature.

Years ago, when I was MD at Rackspace, I visited CibaVision in Portsmouth to see some of the initiatives they'd introduced as part of the Management Today Service Excellence Awards process. They were winners of the B2B category in 2003 and as part of our entry in 2004 we benchmarked ourselves against 26 other firms. They'd handed over control of their all-hands meeting to their team because they'd had feedback from a previous judging round that their comms was all top-down. Management had a slot to deliver its piece, but the rest of the meeting was down to the team. They prepared the agenda and decided what the organisation needed to know. And they had an auditorium where the whole company could gather, with enough chairs for everyone.

Later, when we built the offices for Peer 1, I remembered this. We ensured we had a big space for our monthly all-hands. Our team members agreed on the agenda. They decided what communication was needed. Every session had a Q&A. We even gave out swag for every person who asked a question – sometimes a mousemat, sometimes a hat. A small thing but our team loved it (make sure the stuff you give out is decent, no one likes sh*t swag).

EMBED COMMUNICATION PATTERNS FROM THE BEGINNING

To foster a culture that values open and honest communication, you need to start with new recruits. Tell them they have a superpower. Because they're new to the organisation, they see the world differently and this is something you want to tap into. Every company since Rackspace, I'd give all new joiners a little black book. They were asked to write down anything they noticed that was annoying or stupid about the way we worked. I'd then meet them for lunch regularly during their first six months to discuss their ideas for change or improvement.

This gave a strong message right from the start. It told them that our company valued open communication, from the very top to the very bottom. Their voice was valuable and we wanted to hear it. Proactive communication was important to the business and was a behaviour we wanted to foster. This approach also got people away from the tendency to think that things were someone else's responsibility. And it had the added benefit of making me come over as approachable and engageable – very good characteristics in an MD!

COMMUNICATION CHANNELS

If you have something important to communicate, make sure you choose the right channel. Case in point – one of my clients asked me to look at an email they'd sent out recently. It was long – nearly a side of A4 when you printed it out. The crux of it was that the business was behind on where it needed to be and so changes were going to be made.

Firstly, they hadn't been specific about where they currently were and where they wanted to get to. Whilst the management team knew where the gap was, they didn't communicate the scale of that gap in the email. The team members had jumped to the wrong conclusion immediately and some had started worrying about redundancies. That hadn't been management's intention at all. People will always fill any gaps in knowledge with bad news and rumours can spread like wildfire in this situation.

Secondly, they didn't say when the next update would be coming. This simple addition would have gone a long way towards settling people's nerves.

And thirdly, they didn't say how people could help. The email said, 'We appreciate that you all work hard, but we'd like you to work harder.' For how long? How much harder? Far better to say that this was the focus for the next three months and the target was to move the needle from X to Y. Even better still, they could have said if the company hit that target, there would be a big celebration. As it was, there was no sense of fun, no achievement, no score, no timetable and no way to win. No wonder some of the team were nervous.

Most importantly of all, they'd used email to communicate a really sensitive topic. You need to put yourself in the shoes of the recipient and second guess their reaction. If there's any hint that it might be negative, then think carefully about how you're going to communicate it. The situation I've just described could have been prevented if they'd chosen to make the announcement at an all-hands meeting. When people can see the whites of each other's eyes, they pick up body language and tonality. Management would have had the opportunity to offer clarity and reassurance. And there would have been ample opportunity to discuss any worries in a public forum.

At Peer 1, we were very careful about how we communicated anything controversial. If we thought something could spin out of control (very easy with a team of 660), we jumped on a conference call or video link. This built our organisational memory – everyone knew if things were serious, they needed to get on that call.

KEEP COMMUNICATING

It's not unusual for team members to feel that initiatives are launched with a big fanfare and then they never hear about them again. This leads to a feeling of negativity and a sense of 'Yeah right. Heard it all before'.

The best way to counteract this is to focus on a single theme every quarter. One of my clients had 'Efficiency' for the first quarter of this year. Their goal was to add a couple of percentage points of profit to their bottom line. They zoomed in on their theme with laser precision. Everyone knew that they were looking for efficiency gains and this was communicated and tracked at every daily, weekly and monthly meeting. Their single-minded approach paid off. They achieved their goal a month early.

Bring in some kind of visual reminder that communicates progress with your theme. At Rackspace, we used a Blue Peter style totaliser that was an instant reminder of where we were at. It stimulated conversations about new ways to tackle our goal, other angles to take and initiatives to try. It was a great way to motivate front-line employees. At IT Lab and Peer 1 we tracked all our objectives on TV screens visible from anywhere in the office.

Evidence (or at least folklore) suggests you have to say something seven times before it finally hits home. Seven times! Too often, management will assume that their employees have got the message and get bored well before they reach that seventh repetition.

You need to get creative about repeating things, over and over. Say you've defined your core values. It's not enough to just print them out and stick them on the wall. You need to activate them. Ritz-Carlton Company co-founder Horst Schulze, got his teams to reflect on one of their 24 core behaviours every day in their daily huddle. Only after six months of daily repetition does he feel that it's finally embedded in the organisation. Keep reinforcing your key messages in a rhythmical way and think of new ways to get your message through.

3. RECRUITMENT

I'm going to let you into a secret. There's a method that I've introduced to my CEO clients which they've found transformational. Not only does it massively improve the accuracy of recruitment. It also increases motivation, performance and energy in the business. What is this hard-hitting formula? Creating a job scorecard.

I often talk about the importance of regular talent assessment and ways you could rank team members' performance as A, B and C in your organisation. Your aim has to be getting the percentage of A-Players up to 90% if you can (the definition of an A-Player being the top 10% of the available talent for a given job, salary and location). But in order to do this, you need a structure around job performance and expectations that everyone buys into and accepts. And you need a recruitment process that attracts only A-Players. This is where the job scorecard comes in.

WHAT IS THE DEFINITION OF AN A PLAYER?

A Play·er
/ ā plā-ər/

Noun

Also spelt "A-Player"
- An employee who is in the top 10 percent of their profession on an industry-wide basis for the salary paid.

(Source: 'The A Player' by Rick Crossland)

WHAT IS A JOB SCORECARD?

Creating a job scorecard				
ACTIVITY	TIME	IMPACT	FREQUENCY	MEASUREMENT
TASKS	=5%	H/M/L	D/W/M/A	KPI

Image 3: Job Scorecard Template
Source Monkhouse & Company

Above is the template I use with clients to come up with a job scorecard for every role in their organisation. I suggest this replaces traditional job descriptions, with their endless and overwhelming laundry lists of un-prioritised tasks.

It's simple really. You take each role, whether it's new or existing, and work your way through the grid. First, brainstorm all the tasks this person might be expected to do, even down to making the tea. Can some of these tasks be grouped together? Chunk them up if so. Then work out if any of the tasks you've listed are likely to take up 5% or less of that person's time? Put a line through them.

Begin to pare down to more critical tasks, each one with a percentage of time needed to perform it well. Mark them as high, medium or low impact – prioritising the tasks according to their value to your business. Then decide on the frequency of the task. Is it daily, weekly, monthly or annually?

Maybe you had 20 tasks on the list on the job scorecard when you started but you're aiming to narrow it down to around 5. Then (and this is where the real magic happens), work out the KPI (Key Performance Indicator) that relates to each task. If it's a new role, what would success look like a year from now? If it's a sales role, you may decide that the measure is sales order intake. And the success criteria? How about £10k of monthly recurring revenue in order value by month 12? What is it that they need to do in that task that will mark them out as an A-Player? These can be your measure and benchmark for all future performance discussions. They are also what you look for in interviews.

Ultimately, your organisation needs to get to a place where it's attracting the right skills and everyone knows the expectations of their role. This process goes a long way towards answering the first question of the Gallup Q12 Employee Engagement Survey 'I know what's expected of me at work'. At the end of each day, you want every team member to know whether they've had a good, average or bad day and this information should flow bottom-up from the team.

HOW CAN A SCORECARD HELP WITH RECRUITMENT?

Clients have said to me this has revolutionised the way they think about recruitment. Case in point: a client told me he needed a new salesperson. We went through the job analysis template and by the end, they realised that the tasks split 60% towards management and only 40% towards sales. Clearly, management ability was going to need a much higher profile in the interviews. Going through this process entirely changed their view of what they needed to recruit for.

Other impacts on recruitment include:

* Unifying expectations amongst stakeholders

   At the beginning of any recruitment project, I suggest all the stakeholders gather together and work through the template. As in the example just mentioned, this can radically transform the conversation prior to taking a job to market. All parties can agree what they're looking for based on a clear assessment of the priority of tasks in the job scorecard.

* Bringing clarity into new roles

   Job analysis brings clarity to both candidates and the company. You're focusing on five areas – the most important tasks – and looking for people who have achieved these things to this level in their previous work experience. It's also clear how you're going to measure these things in the role going forward.

Post interview, as each stakeholder discusses their view of the candidate, they can objectively give their thoughts based on his or her ability to deliver the five top priorities to the required standard.

- Showing potential for future development

Now, when a candidate asks you, 'What do I need to do to be successful in this role', you have the answer. The KPIs! It will be crystal clear what they need to achieve to be considered an A-Player in their role.

- Focused job adverts

Your job advert is the first stage of the recruitment and its job is to filter as well as attract. Using a job scorecard cuts through the clutter that often ends up in the ad. It's so specific that you can bring a laser focus to exactly what you're looking for and who should apply.

- Streamlined recruitment process

As with the advert, job analysis can transform the recruitment process. Take the interviews. I have worked with hundreds of clients' employees but only a handful will have had formal interview training. And yet it's fundamental. No-one fails to grasp the impact of hiring the wrong people and yet too little emphasis is given to getting recruitment right. Job analysis is something that you can introduce today that will start having an impact tomorrow. There's no money to spend.

Whether you employ an external recruiter or have an internal interviewing panel, they will go into the interviews with a really clear spec. Questions can be specifically focused on the five task areas of the role and the corresponding KPIs. As a hiring manager, you can get your recruitment team to filter much harder. This has an impact all the way through – fewer CVs and interviews, more thorough screening and only the best candidates being put through. End result? You hire better people. Isn't that the whole point of recruitment?

WHY DO SCORECARDS IMPROVE INTERNAL PERFORMANCE AND ENGAGEMENT?

Once a client is successfully using job analysis in recruitment, I suggest taking it through all levels of their business, starting with the executive team. It works really well if the directors create their scorecards collectively, getting clear on the five things they're counting on each other to do well. They need to think ahead, a year from now, to decide whether they're measuring the right things. Once they're familiar with the process, they can roll it out. This will result in:

- A consistent method for objective assessment, regardless of business size

    Under 100 team members and it's relatively easy for every member of the executive team to tell you their opinion on performance. I remember an executive team who quickly ranked their team – around 50% of their workforce were A-Players.

    However, once the business has grown, it gets far more difficult. As a result, you need to put in a process like job analysis early to provide the data for objective ranking in the future. As mentioned, this information should flow bottom-up from the team themselves as a result of weekly performance conversations.

- Clarity over expectations

I can't over-emphasise the value in every team member knowing what success looks like, how they're going to be measured and how they should spend their time. Let's face it. It's so easy to spend 60% of your time doing email. But this is almost always low impact. By prioritising the important tasks, team members can then time-box their day to ensure they're giving focus to the things that matter.

It's all about expectations. Getting really clear. By working through the job analysis template, both managers and team members can go through an iterative process together. The KPIs are a shared sense of expectation – between the team member and manager, and the whole team. When they start talking about performance, it's based on an objective assessment, not subjective.

As a result of job analysis, every team member will know what they're going to be measured on. One of my clients, Sapphire Balconies, has recently made 'Performance' their quarterly theme. All 75 team members have been taken through job analysis. Now, their Quality department knows that they have to do at least two site visits per day between them. Their KPI is seven site visits a week. Why site visits? Because they've identified these as having the highest impact for their roles. Another employee, a design manager, identified that number one on his priority list is signing off designs on the day they're received. This is because the design team is five hours ahead in India. If this doesn't happen, the project slows down and work grinds to a halt. So this is his top KPI.

- A clear progression path

  Every team member wants to know if they're doing well at something and what they need to do to improve. Now you have a language for coaching conversations based on real, measurable outcomes.

  If you've identified someone as an A-Player, where do they go from there? Well, they should be showing improvement over time on their KPIs. Using a job scorecard gives you a platform. You can lay a path for progression for B-Players or re-align the C-Players who are a good cultural fit, but are falling short on performance. You can't do anything until you know what the problem is. What gets measured gets managed.

- Transparency

  I love the transparency this process brings to the every-day workings of a business. Teams have a new understanding and clarity on their expectations of themselves and each other. It helps them work out their most important areas of focus and provides a mechanism for measuring activity and achievement of objectives.

  Job analysis brings more meaning and structure to the daily huddles that are so vital for forward-movement. It enables team members to identify where they're stuck and how to unblock. Greasing the wheels – that's what it's all about!

- Reduction of friction

  Last, but certainly not least, job analysis will reduce friction and negativity in your business. It's an objective measure of quality – once agreed, it can't be argued with or questioned.

This takes the emotion out of any performance discussions. It's also easier to spot the problems that are holding things back. Maybe it's a CRM system that's rubbish or the phone network needs replacing. Bottlenecks will be more visible, enabling you to minimise 'work in progress'.

When I look back on my early career, I see the moments where this process would have made all the difference to me personally. As a green trainee, straight out of university, I would have avoided the huge embarrassment of failing my first probation meeting. These things live with you forever. I'd thought I was doing ok. I'd had no feedback otherwise. I sat there and was told I was totally sh*t. The shock was so great, I burst into tears (not a good look for a graduate trainee). You owe it to your employees to have job analysis in place.

4. KEEP TEAMS SMALL

Agility. Customer Focus. Passion.

These are the hallmarks of many smaller companies (regardless of the industry). They are fostered by the drive, commitment and energy of their founders. And they're strengthened by the informal, easy communication structure of a small team. But what happens when these companies want to grow?

All too often, organisations lose their way as they begin to scale up. As the number of team members increase, bureaucracy takes hold and stifles energy and creativity. Engagement drops as individuals lose their motivation and start to feel like a faceless number. Hierarchical management structures add to this, breeding a 'them and us' culture that erodes trust and breaks down internal cooperation.

My experience scaling up two firms and coaching many CEOs of other technology businesses has convinced me. If you want to grow, you have to get your structure right from the start. Here's how...

- Size is everything

    As mentioned earlier, there is a hypothesis that the human mind can only handle around 150 relationships simultaneously. As companies get bigger than 150, it's impossible for one person to know everyone individually and understand where they sit in relationship with each other. To my mind, this is when passengers (someone who comes onboard just for the ride, with no intention to do more than the bare minimum the job requires) appear – no-one knows what these people do or can hold them to account.

    W.L. Gore & Associates, the manufacturers of Gore-Tex, run their business on this principle. When a factory expands beyond a team of 150, they feel there are diseconomies of scale. So, they split into two smaller production units. They believe it makes for better communication and a more efficient business.

    Small is beautiful when it comes to team size too. Jeff Bezos, CEO of Amazon, once famously said if a team couldn't be fed with two pizzas, it was too big (although I like Bruce Daisley's swipe at this – he said Bezos was an idiot because everyone knows two pizzas only feeds two people!). I'm a great believer in small teams. No more than 12. Preferably five to nine people. Keeping teams small and agile is, to my mind, one of the keys to unlocking growth.

- Break down tribal boundaries

I believe that your external service will only ever be as good as your internal service. It's vital to fix any silo mentality inside your company because, without this, you'll find it very hard to grow a successful business.

The work of the 1970s psychologist Henri Tajfel illustrates this beautifully. He developed something called social identity theory which said that when we define ourselves, we do so through loyalty to certain groups. Tajfel's experiments showed that humans can enter into 'them and us' thinking in seconds, and they will do so over just about anything.

Tribal thinking is hard-wired into our DNA through millennia of evolution. This can work against you in a corporate culture. To be successful, you'll need to consciously break down tribal divisions between different areas of the business. The aim must be to create customer-focused tribes instead.

A talk I once attended by the Head of Customer Service at TNT gave a great example. He said their customer satisfaction level had been stuck at 95% and wouldn't budge. To find out why, he talked to front line team members. They told him when they wanted to make a promise to a customer, the guys in the depot always said 'no'. There was always a reason why it couldn't be done.

TNT had developed an internal culture that worked to rule because team members didn't have enough direct contact with their customers. As an experiment, all members were given a supply of £5 M&S vouchers. These could be given to any other person who'd been co-operative and helpful. A brilliant scheme! It enabled them to see where the money flowed. Certain teams got most of the money. Their managers had built a culture of 'yes'. This approach enabled TNT to measure internal friction. And they now had a system that reinforced positive behaviour and gave them a mechanism for social currency in the company.

Wherever I've been MD, I've insisted that team members move seats every quarter. This is really powerful. Any 'them and us' negativity between departments melts away. If you try this, be prepared for a backlash. It certainly won't be popular! Mainly because it pushes people out of the comfort and familiarity of their usual surroundings. Team members would complain to me that it was ridiculous. Later, they'd admit they'd been negative because they didn't like someone. But now they were getting on just fine!

PA Consulting told me about a study into the neural networks of companies they had undertaken. They established that six people on a desk will go to six people to get sh*t done. The next desk along might rely on six completely different people. Mix them up and suddenly you've got more options – there are now 12 people they can call on. The more pathways you create, the stronger and more cohesive your organisation. By moving team members around, you'll increase the neural network of your business.

Getting structure right from the very beginning will pay dividends as your company expands. Far better to start on the right footing rather than correcting and restructuring later. Keep teams small and align them with your customers. Stamp on any negativity that builds up between departments and, if necessary, break this down by moving people into different teams. Keep communication channels clear and ensure everyone is truly focused on customer satisfaction. You'll then have solid foundations on which to grow.

5. USE YOUR MANAGERS AS COACHES

Learning, developing, growing – there's a reason these three words go together. You can't have one without the other. They depend on each other. I've worked in businesses that place a high value on coaching and ones that don't. And the ones that don't are the businesses that stagnate.

An organisation's capacity to grow is defined by its openness to learning and this needs to be embedded from the very top to the very bottom. From the CEO to the most junior administrator, there needs to be a commitment to on-going training and personal development.

But why is coaching so important to business growth? And what are its main advantages?

- It's cheap

  Yes – really! A good peer coaching programme will cost nothing but can turn things around really quickly. It shouldn't need specific rules or training. Some of the best I've seen are the simplest. Every team member is allowed to pick someone as their coach or can volunteer to be a coach, agreeing how often to meet. When I'm coaching my clients through this process, I suggest they structure it so that the time commitment is no more than an hour or so every fortnight. This shouldn't be too onerous for any person. Coaching relationships shouldn't last more than 6 months and it's entirely up to the individual whether they want to take part or not. That's the beauty of it. It's not being imposed on you. Take it or leave it!

  However, if the programme isn't working, for either the coach or the coachee, then it needs to stop. Kill it and start again.

I love NextJump's approach to employee development. <u>Harvard Business Review</u> identified them as a DDO (Deliberately Developmental Organisation) and they put strong emphasis on candid feedback. Any perceived weakness that impacts on a team member's ability to do their job is flagged up. They call it your 'backhand' – such a great name.

Opportunities are then created for team members to work on their backhand outside their regular day job. For example, any person who struggles with speaking in public is asked to lead culture tours around the company. By doing this, they deliberately practice their public speaking skills in a way that isn't revenue impacting. Fantastic idea! You can even take their culture tour online.

- Assist in forward planning

In organisations that are scaling quickly, one of the factors that's going to restrain future growth is the availability of more managers. You really need to avoid the trap of promoting someone because they're the least-worst candidate or they've been with you a long time. A person may be a first-rate developer but a lousy manager. Just because they were the first person through the door doesn't mean they should step up into management if they don't have the right skills.

When I work with clients on their strategic goals, we look at projected turnover, future structure, number of team members needed and core capabilities. It's at that moment that the scale of the future problem reveals itself. And that moment when they realise they need to make coaching a priority. A peer coaching programme like the one I've mentioned above could be a good first step. Then I'd recommend a full-blown management development programme to fast track team members who've shown interest.

- Identify your true talent

People who are naturally drawn to management do it instinctively. When I was MD at Rackspace, we hired Lucy who sat next to two of our sales team. One of them, Clarissa, stayed late and came in early to coach her. We didn't ask her to – she just did it. Clarissa had naturally displayed her management tendency. Needless to say, when the promotion came up, it was Clarissa who got it. She turned out to be a superb manager!

It's often the softer skills that are key to good management – and they're the hard skills to measure. It's important to create opportunities for these qualities to shine through – this will help you root out people with potential.

A peer coaching programme will provide these opportunities. Team members can show their mettle around coaching because that's the core skill you want. It will also give your leadership team priceless data on who in the organisation has a growth mindset – whether they're the coach who gets picked more than once or the person who wants to be coached. You'll tap into all that crowd-sourcing information about who it is that the organisation believes has the skills to coach. And if you give participants a 1st, 2nd and 3rd choice of coach you'll get even more valuable data.

So when you do your quarterly talent assessment and analyse who meets or exceeds expectations and who lives by your company values, you'll make judgements based on recent, relevant data.

I'm fascinated by a piece of work Gallup did on self-perception in the workplace. They found that the top quartile of team members (for management ability) know that they're better than some people in their company but don't know how good they are relative to the rest of the universe. On the other hand, the bottom quartile thinks that they're better than average. In other words, the A players don't know they're truly As and the C Players have no idea they're not A Players!

Keep this in mind when people put themselves forward for promotion. They might think they're suitable but often, they're not!

- Drive employee engagement

The Gallup Q12 is a great metric for employee engagement. And if you become a coaching first organisation, it will turbo-charge your score in this test! Increasing engagement can unlock up to 40% more discretionary effort from your team members. Think of that!

Through a peer-coaching programme, you're saying to your team that, 'We value you. Here's your opportunity to develop and grow'. Hopefully, alongside this, you've built a systemic culture of praise and celebration. The coaching programme supports this, providing opportunities for positive feedback and confidence-building. It really is a win-win situation.

- Make employees accountable

By putting the onus on the individual to volunteer to coach or be coached, you're asking them to look at themselves. To think, what is it that I do that I need to get better at, whether that's function-ally or personally, and what are my personal objectives? Team members become accountable for their own development.

Back to NextJump. They give four people group accountability for certain areas of the business. Each of these groups has a captain, two team members and a coach. It's the captain's job to train one of the others to become good enough to be captain, at which point the captain becomes coach. By passing on the baton, they're responsible for replacing themselves. Every manager should see their job in this way. Their goal should be to make themselves redundant so they're ready for the next challenge.

This builds respect and accountability, particularly in bigger companies. It always staggers me how people stop pulling their weight when a business goes over roughly 35 team members. The dirty cups stack up in the kitchen and no-one washes theirs up – so frustrating! These things may seem insignificant but it's an indication there's something else going on. People lose their shared accountability and it starts to become 'someone else's job'.

- Strengthen employee relationships

I'm a great one for building the neural networks of businesses. In the organisations where I've been MD, I've made this a priority. By introducing a peer coaching programme, you'll see new pathways being forged and relationships being strengthened. You can even ensure coaches come from other functional areas or teams to make this aim explicit. It can be powerful for social cohesion in your business.

As well as neural networks, coaching will ensure DNA transfer from old hands to new. This keeps your culture tight. When you're growing, it's easy to lose that founder mentality but here you have a way to retain the essence of your company and ensure everyone understands and feels it.

One of the questions in the Gallup Q12 is around having a best friend at work. It's based on research showing a concrete link between a best friend in the workplace and high performing teams. If you're coaching someone as a peer, there's no management hierarchy. It frees the relationship to focus completely on the individual, without any company agenda or hidden motive. You may see new friendships start to blossom as a result.

Something that worked well with one of my clients was getting all the coaches together at the beginning of the programme so they knew who else was involved. This proved very successful, giving team members the opportunity to ask questions and form their own support network.

Coaching is all about mindset. To become a coaching-first business, everyone needs to understand the importance of learning and growing. It takes deliberate practice and effort before becoming ingrained.

It's not surprising that I feel it's so important – you wouldn't expect anything less from a business coach! But occasionally, I'll come across someone who refuses my help, saying they don't want coaching. That's their decision. But it's like saying you've closed your mind. Ultimately, we never stop learning.

PART 3

THE 10 POINT PLAN FOR SCALING UP YOUR TECHNOLOGY BUSINESS

THE 10 POINT PLAN FOR SCALING UP YOUR TECHNOLOGY BUSINESS

———— * ————

You've decided you want to scale up. You think your business is ready for rapid, significant and sustainable growth. But where do you start? And how do you achieve this goal?

There's no doubt in my mind – scaling up requires a sea change in management thinking and you need to be open to a totally new perspective as well as significant and lasting change. It's all about mindset and deliberate practice. Think about the end state you want. Do you really want your company to be great? Then you need to be prepared to put in the effort and commit to sufficient deliberate practice.

From my experience scaling up two firms and coaching CEOs of other technology businesses, I've identified ten key areas that should be top priorities for any business scale up. Get these areas right and they will be your launch-pad onto an unparalleled growth trajectory. Get them wrong and you're likely to feel stuck and disillusioned.

1. TALENT

Many of my clients tell me that attracting and retaining the right people is one of their biggest challenges. And yet nothing is ever done about it! Keeping the wrong people on your team is like driving around with a flat tyre on your car and never getting it fixed. It couldn't be more important to stop, fix and build a sustainable system to remove the fear of tackling poor performance.

This starts with having the right talent on your leadership team. B Players are not the best available talent for a given salary. Have an action plan to move the % of A-Players upwards each quarter. Sometimes, you have to make tough decisions to replace B Players. Even if you've been working with them for ages.

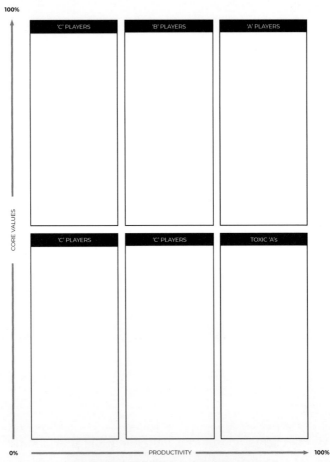

Image 4: Employee Assessment Template
Source Monkhouse & Company

Work out the percentage of your company that are currently A Players and use this as a base-line for future progress. When I start this, it can be anything between 10% and 35% depending on how well the business has been run and how much the wheat has been sorted from the chaff. Often it is on the lower end in firms growing from mergers & acquisitions.

Your aim should be to get this target up to 90%. Having dealt with the C Players, you also need to ensure any B Players only get to stay on if they have the potential to be an A. As you make progress towards this, you'll see a big uptick in recruitment and retention; A Players like to work with fellow A Players so you'll attract and keep the best people.

Sometimes, this process involves some really hard decisions. Take what I call the 'Toxic A Players'. These are people who have particular skills and expertise that are valuable but aren't a good cultural fit. In my experience, they're often salespeople or network engineers. They may be delivering well against their performance targets and the business perceives that it would be hard to replace them. So, they get away with their destructive behaviour.

Sometimes an intervention can work. One of my clients had been having particular problems with a team member for six months. They ended up giving him an ultimatum. Using their core values, they narrowed in on one specific behaviour that was toxic. If it didn't cease, he was out. The person concerned seems to have taken it on board and changed. Time will tell. One thing's for sure, you have to be brutal about this. Just one bad apple can spoil the barrel.

Repeat your talent assessment exercise every quarter, each time tracking your proportion of A Players. Start at the leadership level, move on to managers and look at functional areas and teams. Slice and dice the data however you want.

The first time you do this, it will be top-down. Ultimately, you need to get to a place where the information comes bottom-up. It needs to be rolled out to your organisation in such a way that every person is clear on their individual KPIs. They should be able to measure these themselves every day, week, month and quarter. Their ranking as an A, B or C Player will come from a performance and cultural perspective. And the path towards becoming an A-Player should be crystal clear. They will know what excellence looks like.

Make sure you're not directly measuring people against each other. Each team member should be treated as an individual with their own individual targets. KPIs should be different for each person, based on their expertise, length of service and what they've achieved in the past. This will avoid setting people against each other. It's not a competition, this isn't a forced ranking.

Put in a measure for engagement. The process of regular talent assessment should drive this up. To make your core values and purpose live in your company, make sure you catch people doing the right thing and encourage all team members to give praise and thanks through a values lens.

You can use a system such as Metronome Growth Software to monitor and track all the data needed for your talent assessment. I offer this as part of my service to clients and they find it an easy tool for tracking KPIs, strategy, priorities and metrics.

Finally, put in place a robust recruitment process and measure its effectiveness at every stage. Write decent job ads by working out what you have to offer the A Player you want to attract. Make sure that they are interviewed by other A Players. Spend some time identifying what you're offering – the meaningful work that will motivate them and engage them. Be obsessive – in my experience, CEOs that are obsessive about recruitment are the most successful at scaling up.

2. PURPOSE

As mentioned in Part 1 of this book, having a clear sense of purpose makes companies more successful – fact. In his bestselling book, *'Drive: The Surprising Truth About What Motivates Us'*, Dan Pink identified the secret to high performance and satisfaction, both professionally and personally. He says it's our need to direct our own lives, learn/create new things and do better by ourselves and our world. People want to do work with meaning. This is often associated with younger people, the millennials, but I think it's true of most of us, regardless of how old we are. If you tap into someone's sense of purpose, you'll get much more effort from them.

Once you have a really clear idea of what's driving your company, it can act as a guide, steering you through decisions and keeping you on course. One of my clients, Artemis, a digital marketing agency, decided early on that their purpose is to be 'Champions of Small Businesses'. When their sales teams bring in leads, they ask the question, 'Does this new client fit with our overall purpose?' If they're a big corporation, even though the account may be lucrative, they decide not to take them on. Their purpose has become self-fulfilling.

At Rackspace, we took 'Fanatical Support' through everything, asking ourselves, 'Are we being fanatical enough?' If we identified areas where we fell short, we addressed them. A female graduate we'd just hired told me our maternity package wasn't fanatical enough. We changed it to make it among the best we benchmarked ourselves against. We took our purpose and applied it more broadly, internally as well as externally.

Similarly, your purpose can help you hire people who share your values. It drove our recruitment at both Rackspace and IT Lab. We deliberately looked for people who loved to serve others. And this led us to recruit from different industries – hospitality, retail, security – rather than just the IT sector.

Start with your executive team. What is their personal purpose? What drives them? Your business should facilitate this individual purpose. My work with Cloud-IQ is a great example. As I got their leadership team to open up about their personal motivations, I unearthed a founder's story that hadn't been told. Previously, they'd sat inside a big advertising business, selling software that they felt was designed to rip off their clients. They didn't feel good about this. So eight of them left and set up a new company with a mission to democratise e-commerce. They put a metric around it – they wanted to have given $2 billion back to clients. This gave them a clear vision and an internal brand. It simplified future decision-making as, with a distinct sense of purpose, they knew instantly what the right choice was.

Your customers are human too! If everything your company does is focused in some way on a broader good, it will mean customers will care about you more deeply. At Rackspace, we believed so wholeheartedly in our purpose that we'd happily fix problems that were outside our terms and conditions. For example, when websites were hacked we'd put people on it, night and day, to get it fixed (even though our T&C's said that security and backup was the responsibility of clients). We felt that if we delivered great service, the word would spread and customers would spend more. And they did.

A purpose led, values-driven approach is not for everyone. Some organisations have such ingrained behaviour patterns that they can't or won't change.

But it's within the control of all companies to really define what they're about. As a business coach, I urge clients to give this proper consideration. Re-imagine, capture, create or pull from history what the true purpose of your business is. Then, with this solid foundation, we can move through the rest of my programme, seeing profits rise, employees become happier and businesses grow to realise their full potential.

3. VALUES

My first experience of defining company values came when I was MD at Rackspace. We'd grown to 12 people in the UK and one day, a team member came to me and said, 'You know x? Well, he's useless. He's just not one of us.' This got me thinking – what constituted 'one of us'?

I got the whole team together and told them, instead of negatives, I wanted all the positives. What were the behaviours that we valued at Rackspace? We came up with a list of 14 traits that we wanted to encourage and, from these, whittled down to a set of six company values. Whilst they've evolved over time, the values of Rackspace now are still consistent with these founding principles – 1) Treating Rackers Like Friends and Family 2) Passion For Our Work 3) Committed To Greatness 4) Full Disclosure & Transparency 5) Substance Over Flash 6) Fanatical Support In All We Do.

When I'm coaching clients, I use Jim Collins' 'Mission to Mars' framework – a great approach for defining values. Depending on the size of the company, I start with the executive team then broaden out to management and sometimes the whole team, taking everyone through the same exercise. I get them to imagine we're building an outpost of their company on Mars. But there are only five seats on the rocket-ship. Who would they send? Who best represents the DNA of their company? Who has the highest level of credibility with their peers?

Everyone writes down the names of their five nominations. Once we've reached agreement, we talk about why they've been chosen. What are the behaviours they exhibit? Having pinpointed this list, we boil them down, defining the core values at the heart of these traits.

Everyone in your organisation needs to live and breathe your values. Don't just include them on your website and marketing literature. Put them up on the wall. Add them to all your documentation, your security passes, anything that will reinforce the message. When you see someone displaying a behaviour linked with your values, single them out and offer praise.

At Rackspace, we always gave praise through a values lens. If we caught someone doing the right thing, we'd say thanks then write it on a post-it note and stick it on the wall, right next to the value they'd embodied. Kudos and social currency were doled out according to Rackspace values. In monthly all-hands meetings, team leaders would stand up and give bottles of champagne to people outside their team who'd enabled them to deliver outstanding service. Our employee of the month and quarter were chosen by the team based on our values.

It's really important to ensure all your team members are a values-fit. You need to be clear about the behaviours you want to see otherwise you won't be able to hire for them. Once you have the list, it simplifies recruitment, making it consistent across disciplines. You're only looking for people that exhibit and evidence these behaviours.

As MD of Peer 1, I made sure our values were at the heart of our performance development process. In our leadership maturity model, team members could be a 'player, coach, master or guru' against each of our values. If you ranked as a 'player', you were exhibiting the behaviour that links to the value well enough, but

you could be doing it better. This gave a clear idea about personal
development and direction for improvement.

Value	Player	Captain	Coach	Master
Every Interaction Matters	Engages in high impact conversations (listening, test assumptions, 100% accountability, and vs. but, direct conversations)	Builds high performance teams	Fosters cross-functional collaboration	Creates a high performance, highly engaged culture
	Focuses on the customer as a person (not revenue)	Understands and anticipates customers needs (int and ext)	Skillfully addresses customer challenges	Brings a strategic perspective to emerging customer needs (forward planning)
Enable Others to Succeed	Seeks feedback from PEERs ; offers feedback to PEERs.	Delivers development feedback to reports and team	Coaches individuals and team towards high performance	Constantly scans, identifies and eliminates organizational barriers to success
	Self-awareness: aware of own strengths and limitations. Leaves ego at the door	Acknowledges and capitalizes on individual strengths in team	Facilitates results through aligning skills, abilities and strengths of individuals and teams	Identifies trends and opportunities for increasing organizational capability
Strive for Excellence	Focuses on results by creating individual performance and leadership goals	Focuses the team on results by creating shared goals, objectives and metrics for the team	Identifies and leverages x-functional interdependencies to achieve results	Establishes stretch goals and provides strategic vision for the company as a whole
	Admits and Learns from mistakes	Debriefs and facilitates learning from mistakes	Identifies and addresses systemic and human implications for mistakes	Creates a culture of learning where it is safe to take risks and learn from mistakes
Anything in Possible	Innovates: Looks for opportunities to improve experience for PEERs and customers	Is willing to take risks and challenge the status quo; Offers solutions.	Drives the implementation of change to improve performance	Champions change and creates an environment for new ideas to thrive
	Looks for creative solutions for day-to-day challenges	Creates team atmosphere of possibility (say yes and figure out the "how")	Aligns teams towards strategic vision of the future	Inspires team to feel a sense of purpose
Sense of Fun and Play	Recognizes and appreciates the work and efforts of co-workers	Celebrates team's successes and milestones	Recognizes contribution of PEERs across the organization	Creates a culture of recognition and celebration
	Creates own definition of balance	Works with team to balance results with personal sustainability; shows care and empathy	Creates and designs work arrangements that maximize performance and sustainability of team members	Builds a culture that considers health and wellbeing of all employees

Image 5: Values-Based Leadership Maturity Model
Source: Peer1 Hosting 2011

When we were still small at Rackspace, we scored everyone against our values every quarter. The person with the highest score was then de facto employee of the quarter and I'd speak directly to anybody with low scores. I remember vividly one guy, David, who scored at the very bottom one particular quarter. The feedback I gave him was, 'Really sorry you're at the bottom but you didn't pick the phone up quickly enough and that's really annoying everyone on your team.' Next quarter, bang! He came first, winning employee of the quarter. He'd been given simple, direct feedback that he acted on straightaway. These days I sum this up as giving people radically candid feedback.

A good set of values can help with workforce planning. Every quarter, rank everyone in your organisation against them. Decide whether they are a fit, meeting your values or falling short. You need to get everyone up to an A. It must be your aim to only employ A Players – the top 10% of available talent for a given salary, in your location, for that particular job. Remember, A Players are going to give you 10x or even 20x more for roughly the same salary.

Here are some thoughts from Steve Jobs on the impact of hiring A Players:

"I observed something fairly early on at Apple, which I didn't know how to explain then, but I've thought a lot about it since. Most things in life have a dynamic range in which [the ratio of] "average" to "best" is at most 2:1. For example, if you go to New York City and get an average taxi cab driver, versus the best taxi cab driver, you'll probably get to your destination with the best taxi driver 30% faster. And an automobile; what's the difference between the average car and the best? Maybe 20%? The best CD player versus the average CD player? Maybe 20%? So 2:1 is a big dynamic range for most things in life.

Now, in software, and it used to be the case in hardware, the difference between the average software developer and the best is 50:1; maybe even 100:1. Very few things in life are like this, but what I was lucky enough to spend my life doing, which is software, is like this. So I've built a lot of my success on finding these truly gifted people, and not settling for "B" and "C" players, but really going for the "A" players. And I found something... I found that when you get enough "A" players together, when you go through the incredible work to find these "A" players, they really like working with each other. Because most have never had the chance to do that before. And they don't work with "B" and "C" players, so it's self-policing. They only want to hire "A" players. So you build these pockets of "A" players and it just propagates."

Once you've decided and agreed your values, recognise that they're not set in stone. You need to assess whether they're useful and working. Review them every quarter, checking that they're guiding your recruitment and performance development. They really should be a compass or north star that's leading your business forwards.

After review, if you feel a particular value isn't right or working well for your company, cull it or refine it down into something that's more meaningful to your team. Less is more.

Finally, resist the temptation to use words like teamwork, ethical or excellence as your values. Try this test. If you read your list of values would it identify your firm in your industry or could it be any of your competitors as well? You are looking for a distinctive set of words – your choice of language is important. In its annual report to shareholders, Enron listed its core values as follows: Communication – We have an obligation to communicate. Respect – We treat others as we would like to be treated. Integrity – We work with customers and prospects openly, honestly, and sincerely.

Values are the essence of your company's identity. They communicate what's important to you and define your organisational culture. But they're only truly valuable if they're deeply embedded in the way you do business, interact with others, recruit, develop and grow. Having a set of shared values that everyone buys into will help you shape a strong culture. This will then energise teams, increase productivity and ultimately drive growth.

4. PRINCIPLES

Bureaucracy – how I hate that word! Get rid of stupid rules that irritate and frustrate your teams. Set up a special email address and ask them to tell you whenever they come up against something that doesn't make sense. It amazes me how many crazy rules are written for the 2% of the time that a single person transgressed once, annoying 98% of those who have never and will never do that particular thing.

Come up with a new set of principles that are linked to your values. Statements about how every person is going to behave as opposed to strict rules. For example my three principles are 1) if in doubt, do the right thing, 2) it's better to seek forgiveness than ask permission and 3) don't bring me a problem without a solution (because that would be whinging). Keep it simple and make sure everyone knows and understands them.

When I was at Rackspace, I was introduced to The Rockefeller Habits, which were instrumental in pushing the company into stratospheric growth. The Rockefeller Habits were Rackspace's Chairman's preferred execution framework for scaling up, so I got first hand experience of using them. I was blown away on how using them allowed us to focus on the things that mattered and so I brought them to both IT Lab and Peer 1. Today they are the basis of my coaching practice, and I introduce all clients to them.

It would be no exaggeration to say Verne Harnish's book, *'Mastering the Rockefeller Habits: What You Must Do to Increase the Value of Your Growing Firm'* has changed my life. Here are the Habits in a nutshell:

1. THE EXECUTIVE TEAM IS HEALTHY AND ALIGNED

This is number one for a reason, the rest can be tackled in any order. This is the fundamental building block to success because your company will never perform better than its leadership team. Everything comes down from the top so you need to spend time and resources on getting this right.

2. EVERYONE IS ALIGNED WITH THE #1 THING THAT NEEDS TO BE ACCOMPLISHED THIS QUARTER TO MOVE THE COMPANY FORWARD

This is all about focus and clarity. Drill down into the practicalities of how to achieve your goal and keep drilling down until you've got to what you're going to do today and tomorrow. That's the level of detail you need and then a single person needs to be accountable for completing these actions.

Make sure that your theme for the quarter means something and benefits both your team and your customers. For example, you may decide you want to improve the customer experience around a particular product because you know this would reduce the inbound volume of customer complaints. This would then free up 20% of your team's time which you could allocate to learning and development. Tell this good news story so people can see how everything links together.

3. COMMUNICATION RHYTHM IS ESTABLISHED AND INFORMATION MOVES THROUGH THE ORGANISATION ACCURATELY AND QUICKLY.

Rhythm is so important. Daily, weekly, monthly, quarterly – set a meeting cycle and commit to it. If your teams are meeting in a daily huddle, they get the chance to share, collaborate and build trust. You're looking for the stucks that come up time and time again. These are the things that are getting in the way of your organisation moving forwards.

4. EVERY FACET OF THE ORGANISATION HAS A PERSON ASSIGNED WITH ACCOUNTABILITY FOR ENSURING GOALS ARE MET

Accountability is a vital component for growth in The Rockefeller Habits. One person is all too often in multiple boxes. One function is being covered by a number of people, so no-one is really doing it well. It needs to be assigned. This gives clarity for who has overall accountability for each step.

5. ONGOING TEAM INPUT IS COLLECTED TO IDENTIFY OBSTACLES AND OPPORTUNITIES

Managers should collect team members input, week in, week out. Regular one-to-ones throughout the month will allow for feedback in both directions about progress and development. Your executive team needs to commit to talking to at least one person from a different team every week. Being able to share conversations with people on the front line will create a much more informed executive meeting! This will give a much better overview of the stucks and enable you to get the sand out of people's shoes much quicker.

6. REPORTING AND ANALYSIS OF CUSTOMER FEEDBACK DATA IS AS FREQUENT AND ACCURATE AS FINANCIAL DATA

My preferred measure for customer satisfaction is Net Promoter Score (NPS). It's a perfect metric, enabling you to grow your business through word of mouth. By implementing this and running it on a quarterly and annual cycle, you can keep tabs on your company's performance and have accurate data when you most need it.

7. CORE VALUES AND PURPOSE ARE ALIVE IN THE ORGANISATION

Alive is the key word here. Many organisations spend time coming up with core values and then put them on some literature or on the wall and forget about them. Very few will actually 'live' them. Make sure that the core values are built into hiring, firing and promotion. Use them to give praise as well as reprimands. Include them in the everyday vocab of your company.

8. EMPLOYEES CAN ARTICULATE THE KEY COMPONENTS OF THE COMPANY'S STRATEGY ACCURATELY

The key components here are the BHAG, the Core Customer and the Three Brand Promises. Lots of companies I speak with about Mastering the Rockefeller Habits say they don't have a BHAG. But it's so important for engagement, focus and motivation in your teams. Often, they also say they don't have one core customer. In fact, they have several!

Defining your brand promises, with their corresponding guarantees, is incredibly powerful. At Rackspace, our brand promises were 1) 'Zero downtime network' 2) 'Answer the phone in 3 rings or less' and 3) 'Fix your hardware in under 4 hours'. If we failed to deliver it cost us money. This was our catalytic mechanism of guarantee for our clients – our skin was in the game.

9. ALL EMPLOYEES CAN ANSWER QUANTITATIVELY WHETHER THEY HAD A GOOD DAY OR WEEK

One of the key elements in Mastering the Rockefeller Habits is every team member being able to answer question 1 of Gallup's Q12 – Do you know what is expected of you at work? Seldom do I find an organisation where this is true. Measuring engagement in team members – another of my big pieces of advice - is so important. I always advise using the Gallup Q12 for this. It's such a good tool. People need to know what's expected of them at work and this needs to be linked to OKRs, objectives and measurable key results, that tie in with the overall theme for the quarter.

10. THE COMPANY'S PLANS AND PERFORMANCE ARE VISIBLE TO EVERYONE

Make sure you have a system in place for tracking. Successful companies have scoreboards everywhere – monitors in reception, screens showing results, totaliser boards. They come up with inventive ways to display their core values, making sure they're not annoying or hackneyed.

At Rackspace, we created a logo for each one of our values. If we caught someone doing the right thing, we'd say thanks then write it on a post-it note and stick it on the wall, right next to the value they'd embodied.

5. ENGAGEMENT

I'll say it until you're bored of listening. Happy employees + happy customers = profitability. Simple! I think that's all any successful business needs. Through my career as Managing Director of three technology companies, this has been my guiding principle. So much so, that I believe everyone else must think the same. Not so.

However, through coaching others, I found that the majority of companies in the room have no handle on their team or customer engagement. That's crazy!

Regular, systematic measurement of engagement is essential to your company's future growth and prosperity. Here are 6 reasons why:

- It acts as an early warning system for your business

    Put in place decent metrics and you'll have an efficient early warning system to alert you to any issues with team members or customers before they do too much damage. Instead of waiting for an annual appraisal or customer survey, you can sort things out quicker.

    At Rackspace, we were growing fast. We needed something to help us maintain the clarity of communication and satisfaction levels that we'd enjoyed as a small start-up. So we ran the Gallup Q12 annually across the whole company and quarterly within teams. This enabled us to keep a close eye on all areas of the business. Since ITLab, I have also gathered a weekly pulse on team member engagement. My tool of choice for this comes from Nic Marks at fridaypulse.com.

    Following this, I put in the Net Promoter Score as a measure for customer satisfaction. By implementing this and running it on a quarterly cycle, you can keep tabs on your company's performance and have accurate data when you most need it.

- It removes corrosive attitudes

    Have you ever felt you're doing a good job but people around you don't care? Or that you're working harder than someone else but being paid the same? How did that make you feel? It's so easy for resentful, corrosive attitudes to set in and spread like wildfire. This is why you need input/output metrics to measure performance against the values you think are important. And everybody needs to know and understand these metrics.

They encourage clarity and transparency. If you share KPIs, everyone knows what everyone else's goals are. Introduce salary bandings as well, showing different levels within each job role. Then people will know what they need to do to get more money or develop further. Suddenly, the resentment and tension melts away.

- It identifies issues with management

Managers account for at least 70% of variance in employee engagement, Gallup estimates.

When we merged ServerBeach into Peer 1, we asked the whole team, 'If you could run the business for a day, what would you do differently?' We thought they'd say they wanted more money or training. But you know what? They overwhelmingly said they'd like to work with better people. We knew we had work to do with our middle managers!

When you get past 30 people in the business, you're no longer an owner/founder interacting regularly with all your team members. It's more likely that their experience of your company will revolve around working for one of your managers. This is why you, as owner/founder, have got to stay on top of the recruitment process to make sure only good people get in. You'll want to promote your managers from within. Your best salesperson might become Head of Sales or your best Dev guy could become Head of Development, but you need to know whether they are having a positive or negative impact on team members.

Some of the Gallup questions relate particularly to managers. Although the surveys are anonymous, respondents can say where they fit into the organisation. You'll get a sense of whether engagement is being hindered or driven by frontline management. And then you can do something about it. If great managers seem scarce, it's because the talent required to be one is rare. Gallup's research reveals that only one in ten people possess the talent to manage.

- It motivates employees and customers

The first question on the Gallup Q12 is important. 'I know what's expected of me at work'. I don't think most people get up every morning and say, 'I'm going to do a sh*t job today.' They want to feel they're making progress, growing and doing well. So you need to put in place metrics to ensure they're clear on what 'good' looks like.

Quarterly OKRs and KPIs are essential along with a system where team members can see how they are personally making a contribution. Come up with a leading indicator (e.g. hours on phone, numbers of meetings, numbers of proposals) and a lagging indicator (e.g. revenue in the sales team). At Rackspace we worked out that every minute our salespeople spent on the phone correlated with £1 of monthly recurring revenue. Once we had this, we could track it on a board. You could see your cumulative hours and strive towards your target. This also gave crystal clear focus to what was important in your workload.

Having these systems in place means every team member knows what's expected of them. They themselves can keep score. And they never get to the point at the end of the year when they're asking their manager, how did I do?

Games have rules, white lines and scores. How many golfers get no better over time? Most? That's the contrast of just playing the game versus deliberately practising. To get better over time, the team needs to deliberately practice and know the score in real time. Not just the rules and the white lines.

Similarly, a regular feedback mechanism for customers will encourage better loyalty. When I first joined IT Lab, our NPS was -5. Two years later, we'd got it up to +55. Every quarter, we'd write to customers telling them about the feedback we'd been given and what we'd done about it. This showed that, instead of paying lip service, we were listening and improving. Closed-loop feedback meant they were more likely to engage in giving further feedback.

We also invited our top 25 customers onto a steering board, asking for their views to help improve our business. This resulted in stronger emotional bonds and loyalty from the small number of customers that were responsible for the majority of our revenue.

- It gives an external benchmark

If you use Gallup to run your Q12, they'll put your results into the context of engagement levels in similar companies. External benchmarks can be pretty useful. In 2005 Rackspace won a Service Excellence Award from Management Today. In 2006 Rackspace was the best small IT company to work for in the Best Companies™ awards published in the Sunday Times.

That same year we had benchmarked 26 different companies who had ranked highly as great places to work. We had sent out teams to visit them and bring back ideas. Every 6 months or so, we'd also get visits from organisations keen to see what we had done. Our team members loved this – they'd see them walking around and feel proud to share.

One year, we were nominated for a European award. We asked the whole team, 'Who has made the biggest contribution towards making Rackspace a great place to work in the last year?' The result? Overwhelmingly – Sam and Annalize. So we sent those two to the ceremony in Copenhagen and they came back brimming with even more ideas for team motivation!

- It shows employees and customers you care

The Gallup question that provokes the most hilarity is 'I have a best friend at work'. Gallup included this as they found it was a characteristic of high performing teams. We were really hot on this at Rackspace. When Sam and Annalize came back from Copenhagen, they said they wanted to be 'fluff fairies'. Come again? They wanted to secretly spread a little fluff amongst the Rackspace team!

They made it their mission to know when a team member was having a tough time. And they'd do something anonymously to help. One time, there was an ex-pat that needed to go home at short notice for a family emergency but it was the school holidays and the flights were too expensive. Next thing she knew, the fluff fairies had paid a surprise visit to her desk. She came in to see fairy dust all over her keyboard and underneath it, an envelope containing flight tickets. She was over the moon. You couldn't get more caring than that.

We would also go out of our way to remove little annoyances and irritations that drain energy and engagement. New team members were given a little black book. We told them we valued their fresh perspective and asked them to write down anything, no matter how small, that seemed odd or stupid. We also had an open email address and gave a £10 Amazon voucher to anyone who flagged up stupid rules or suggested a way we could improve. And we acted on as many of these suggestions as possible.

All these measures ensured team churn was kept at a healthy level, which also helped us retain our customers. On top of this, the directors would personally ring any customer who'd given us a detractor score in their NPS and would close the loop by feeding back to them afterwards.

Measurement of engagement in team members and customers is critical to your company's success. Studies have shown a direct link between high levels of engagement and business results. And you won't know if you're on track without regular, systematic measurement. You need to create a culture that seeks criticism. If you can achieve that magic balance between a happy team and happy customers, then everything else will fall into place. Your vision for a growing, profitable business will start to become a reality.

6. CANDOUR

Telling it straight. Being open and honest. Giving constructive guidance and feedback. They all sound simple but are, in fact, really hard. For many people, being direct and confronting difficult issues pushes them right out of their comfort zone. Add to this our good old British reserve and you often find that companies in the UK are hotbeds for negative gossip, backstabbing and mistrust.

There's a huge crisis in trust globally. In 1976, trust in the media was at 76%. Today it's at 32%. Trust in office communications is at an equivalent all-time low. And, with only 19% of millennials believing that 'most people can be trusted', it's not looking set to improve any time soon.

If there's a problem with trust in your company, know this. It's likely to be costing you the most money. Lack of trust is corrosive, causing fragmentation, division and unhappiness. Productivity drops along with levels of engagement. So, if you're serious about growing your business, you need to get this sorted quickly. You won't get anywhere without trust. But how do you build it into your company?

- Start with Salaries

  Salary transparency. Really? I can sense your heart filling with dread. And yet, if you want to get to the root of any negativity in your organisation, this is a good place to start. Secrecy in companies can be corrosive, particularly around this issue. So, take the opposite view. Only keep things secret when you absolutely have to.

  Ask yourself why you might feel threatened by salary transparency. Is it because you know there's an inherent unfairness in your business? Then fix this straightaway. Running a business on lies is not a good premise for success. Isn't it only right that two people doing the same job should be paid the same salary? What is your gender pay gap?

  One of the things I suggest to my clients is to introduce job families. It's a good first step towards salary transparency and something we introduced when I was MD at IT Lab. Grouping roles and then giving them a salary band will enable team members to know what skills, experience and values-led behaviours they need to demonstrate before they get a pay rise. Introducing different levels within these job families gives team members something to aim for. It also provides an easily justifiable reason why some people are getting paid more than others. And your managers need to commit to coaching to facilitate progression within their teams.

Makers Academy went a step further and allowed team members to set their own salaries. They believe this is fundamental to building trust between colleagues. The only time the company decides salary levels is when people are first recruited. The moment someone's hired, their offer letter appears on the company intranet. Everyone knows what they're being paid. And if someone feels they're worthy of a pay rise, there's a process to follow.

First, they write an essay giving their reasons why – the value they feel they bring to the company, the market-testing they've done externally etc. Four colleagues are then chosen to peer review this essay. Once it's agreed, the request goes straight to Finance who sanction the pay rise. This approach encourages self-awareness, takes away the traditionally adversarial nature of pay reviews and facilitates the giving and receiving of feedback between the whole team.

- Hire Truthfully

When I recruit team members, I always look for people with curiosity and coachability at interviews. As a test, I give radically candid feedback to applicants. They need to be able to take it – this tells you a lot about someone. I'll chat away with them and then ask them why they haven't done up their top button. Or brought a pad and pen. Or had a shave! Occasionally, someone gives a good answer. One guy told me his hairdresser thought he looked sexier with a day's growth. He had a date later on so hadn't shaved for the interview. He wasn't offended by my frankness and was prepared to be vulnerable. Needless to say, I hired him.

Give open, honest feedback to any unsuccessful candidates. Tell them why you didn't hire them. It shows that you care about them finding a job elsewhere. If you've made it easier for them next time, you've created a benefit through the hiring process. Many managers won't do this as it makes them uncomfortable. But your feedback is much more likely to be appreciated than not.

- Leadership should live and breathe it

If you want to properly embed honesty and candour throughout your company, it has to come from the top. Your Senior Leadership Team needs to decide it will not accept any triangulation. Ideally, do this six months ahead of the rest of the company. Agree that you won't have any negative conversations about anyone else unless they're in the room. Commit to open, honest communication and peer coaching. Work on confrontation, battle against the stiff upper lip of Britishness and make transparent, open communication the norm. Monitor each other and don't introduce it anywhere else until you've all agreed you're doing it correctly. You'll be amazed how it starts to filter out naturally to the rest of the organisation if you're modelling it well. It will become the way you operate, every day.

And if someone in your senior leadership team can't commit to this? Then they have no place in your company. You're trying to drive behavioural change to create a high performing team. You need total buy-in.

- Seek Criticism

  As a boss, I want my team to feel they can speak truth to power. In the same way as I want to be honest with them, I want them to be honest with me. Without constructive criticism, how will a company ever improve and grow? At the various companies where I've been MD, I've encouraged team members to tell me when there are stupid rules or habits that have crept in under the radar. It's important not to take any of this personally but use it to make things better. Build a culture where you value people's opinions and act on their concerns.

  This goes for customers too. I've used Net Promoter Score not because we wanted to pat ourselves on the back for being brilliant. We were actively seeking criticism from our detractors. This told us where we needed to improve and helped us focus on the things that mattered.

- Show that you care

  When I'm coaching clients, I like to ask them some revealing questions. If a colleague has spinach in their teeth, would they tell them? Maybe two thirds of hands go up in the room. I then ask them, how about if another colleague has come into work with really bad BO? Or bad breath? Would they still tell them? By now, most of the hands in the room are down. We naturally find these sorts of conversations uncomfortable.

  And yet, I ask them, if you yourself had spinach in your teeth or BO that you weren't aware of, wouldn't you prefer that someone told you? Rather than walking around all day with people talking about you behind your back? If you really care about the person, you should be honest and tell them. If you can't do this for them, then how are you going to tell them they're not great at their job?

This is the essence of 'Radical Candour', a phrase coined by Kim Scott in her best-selling book. Her pivotal moment came when she was given brutally honest feedback by Sheryl Sandberg when she was working at Google. After a presentation that had gone well, Sandberg took her aside. She congratulated her but then told her she'd said 'um' a lot. To drive the point home, she said this made her sound less smart, even though she very obviously wasn't, and suggested she see a speech therapist to fix it. When Kim reflected on this encounter, she defined her theory of radical candour – a skill that requires bosses simultaneously to care personally whilst challenging their team members directly.

Creating a culture with honesty and openness at its core is difficult. But if you can make radical candour the default way in which your organisation behaves, you'll have done something that's really transformational. It will pay dividends every, single day – like compound interest for your organisation. You'll move faster and grow quicker with way less organisational drag and bureaucracy holding you back. For the vast majority of individuals, being radically candid is going to be uncomfortable but stick with it. Tell them why it's important and train the behaviour into the organisation.

7. MEETINGS

James Tiberius Kirk, Captain of the USS Enterprise got it so right: *"A meeting is an event where minutes are taken and hours wasted."*

Have you ever felt like you've wasted your time by being in a meeting? I bet there isn't anyone who wouldn't put their hand up for that one. In fact, when I'm working with a group of people or speaking in public, I often ask that question and everybody does give an emphatic "yes". We've all experienced frustration of some kind while in a meeting, and we all know the joke that meetings are the only paid alternative to working for a living.

Why don't people, and organisations, do something about it? Perhaps it's because there are some norms of behaviour in the organisation that say this is how we run our meetings, and you can't change it. But we should be able to change it. Who wants to waste their time sitting in a meeting they don't need to be at? Or one that has no point to it?

Here's a simple framework that can be used for meetings where you're trying to solve some kind of organisational problem. I know this won't work for all standing meetings (huddles, all-hands etc) but many of the ideas transfer:

- The invitation

  When an invitation is sent it gives people context. Tell them what the meeting is for, what will be covered and what you want to achieve. Then people can look at that and understand why it is they're invited. Or, if they don't think they need to be there, they don't need to accept! I know people don't always feel they can do that, so I say to clients make it a social norm in your organisation that attendance is optional.

- The rule of 7

  Try to keep the number of people in the meeting to as few as possible to achieve the desired outcome. The book, 'Decide & Deliver: 5 Steps to Breakthrough Performance in Your Organization', says that once you've got seven people in a group, each additional member reduces decision effectiveness by 10%. If you run above 7 you're then into communication rather than decision making. Let's try to keep meetings small.

- Start with good news

  We want to create a safe place for people to speak out. They need to feel they can say what they want, and one way of doing that is by getting everyone to share some good news right at the start of the meeting. Get off to a good start with positive news. This helps create Psychological Safety which, according to Google's Project Aristotle research, is the main component of effective teams. They write: *"Psychological safety refers to an individual's perception of the consequences of taking an interpersonal risk or a belief that a team is safe for risk taking in the face of being seen as ignorant, incompetent, negative, or disruptive. In a team with high psychological safety, teammates feel safe to take risks around their team members. They feel confident that no one on the team will embarrass or punish anyone else for admitting a mistake, asking a question, or offering a new idea."*

- Set rules

  Each organisation should have a clear definition of how it runs meetings. Are you allowed to do your shopping online and pay no attention to what's being said? If you're not in the meeting to catch up on emails or to write a shopping list, then the rule should be no tech allowed.

  If you've got to run a conference call then use video conferencing. If you know people can see what you're up to it stops the attention wandering and drives better, shorter meetings.

  Don't we all know that one person who, in every meeting, takes over. They love the sound of their own voice and don't give anyone else a chance to speak, so instead of letting that happen each time what about a rule giving everyone equal airtime. Another extract from Google's research is that the best teams allow all participants to have their say. One of the roles of the chair or facilitator is to ensure that this unusual habit becomes the norm.

Sometimes you'll find people talking about things that aren't on the agenda. A way to stop that is to reaffirm what is to be covered within the time available. This can be done after giving the 'good news'. Get agreement on the context of the meeting and then ensure all items to be discussed are clearly on the agenda. If you have something you want to cover, put it on the agenda at the beginning. I know you've already set out what you want to accomplish in your original invitation, but let's go back over it because things may have changed since the invitation was sent. It might be that a different problem needs solving. Prioritise the items. Cover the most pressing first. Once that's all done get a commitment from everyone in the room that they are going to participate fully.

• Set roles

Facilitating a meeting successfully is a skill so don't automatically make the person who called the meeting the chair or facilitator (whatever your organisation calls that person). The person who called the meeting may be rubbish at taking the lead or might want to be an active participant (it's tough to facilitate and participate), so pick the best person or rotate to give everyone experience.

Find yourself a *note taker* who can take notes for everyone. Someone who can update One Note, Google Docs (whatever shared system you use) live as the meeting progresses. This way people know where to find the information once it finishes. During the meeting, everyone can focus on the discussion.

It might be worthwhile thinking about whether you want to record the meeting. Ray Dalio, the American billionaire investor of Bridgewater Associates, videos every meeting. Some organisations record audio. It just means that if there is ever a debate or a discussion about who said what you can go back and find it. Or if a meeting didn't go as planned you can rerun the tape and learn from the experience.

Make sure you have a *timekeeper*. You need to start and finish on time (because a lot of the time they don't, and it's annoying). You need to make sure you finish in time for feedback, which brings me nicely onto.....

- Rate the meeting

  Always leave time at the end of the meeting for people to give feedback. On a scale of one to ten, how would you rate this meeting? What feedback would you give to participants? Is it thumbs up, or thumbs down — and why? This will help to improve meetings for next time. Did the facilitator do a great job or not? Give them some feedback.

- Respect people's time

  I think I've spent large tranches of my life in meetings I didn't need to be in. Or sometimes I would need to be there for a small part, and the rest was of no interest to me. So, maybe we need to make sure people know they can leave if they want to. If they've covered their part, and the rest is no longer relevant, they can go because we recognise they've got other stuff they could be doing. We respect their time. And if you're needed for agenda item number 6, but not before, ask for someone to message you when it's nearly time for that part of the meeting, and come back. There's no point sitting through 40 minutes of stuff you're not interested in!

Elon Musk is of the same opinion. He wrote a memo to all his employees at Tesla Motors and it included the advice: *"Walk out of a meeting or drop off a call as soon as it is obvious you aren't adding value. It is not rude to leave, it is rude to make someone stay and waste their time"*.

- 50 minute meetings

Why do nearly all organisations usually set meetings for an hour? If I've got back to back meetings, how am I physically going to get from one to the other, when one finishes at midday and the other begins at midday? Unless they're in the same room. But even then, that extra ten minutes allows you time to check up on emails (remember we've got a rule for no tech so you haven't checked them in a while), or just go to the toilet!

- The issues list

Sometimes we just don't have enough time to get through everything on the agenda. In those cases, the leftovers can be moved to the 'issues list'. It's a list of items that still need to be resolved and we can talk about next time. They may even become separate meetings in their own right.

I know many other people might add "follow up" onto the end of this list, but I won't. If the note taker is writing everything down as we go along, and saving it to a shared system, we can all look at that afterwards. And, if someone says they will do something by a certain time, it's their job to do it. Trust them.

8. RHYTHM

Every business has its own rhythm. Whether it's meetings, goals, budgetary cycles or communication frequency – all can be influenced and controlled for optimal efficiency. Like the conductor of the finest orchestra, as CEO you can listen critically, tune, adjust tempo and control dynamics to create a perfect performance. Your aim? To manage the energy of your business in a positive and productive way. I often refer to the CEO as the chief energy officer for this reason.

To do this requires sustained effort and consistent application – everyone needs to feel the beat and stay in time. If you're looking to scale up, getting the right rhythm in place from the start is vital.

I personally don't think annual rhythms work. A quarterly cycle is much more effective, both in terms of performance development and goal setting. Take annual appraisals (my pet hate!). If you're thinking of introducing them, don't! Get rid of them if they already exist in your company. They're useless. If you're a manager, you should be giving weekly feedback to your team.

The same goes for annual budgeting. Too often I've witnessed finance teams inventing arbitrary numbers out of thin air. If budgets are measured annually, there's little scope for adjustment. Worse, if team members know after 6 months that they're on course to hit their annual target, they'll take their foot off the gas. Far better to create meaningful ratios or percentages that are measured on a quarterly cycle. When I was MD at Peer 1, we took this approach. For example, our customer experience team was given a budget of 5% of revenue. As we knew likely revenue for the next quarter, this team could make definite plans based on realistic figures.

Time and again, I've seen how a 90-day rhythm can build alignment in a business. Teams feel most engaged when they know what's expected of them. If it's made clear to them, they'll know that what they've done has made a difference and it's been meaningful. It's far easier to see the link between what you do today and a quarterly theme as you can see and make sense of a nearer horizon. Think weekly check-ins on the Blue Peter totaliser rather than playing for a year and finding out the score months after the game finished.

Quarterly kickoffs are a good place to start when your 90-day theme is clearly communicated and linked to the longer-term vision. Every team member should select three or four stretch objectives and key results linked to the 90-day theme. They should then discuss these in a 'daily huddle', talking through what they did yesterday, what they did today, what are the 'blockers' or alerts for the team to look out for etc.

I've found team members often push back on the daily huddle. They say they don't have time, or it doesn't add any value. I say, if it doesn't add value, you're not doing it right! It shouldn't last more than 15 minutes, you should huddle standing up and you should start with some good news. Your entire team needs to realise that if they take 15 minutes out of their day, every day, they will get back so much more from the clarity of overcoming hurdles and agreeing on priorities. They will feel more connected to the business and the people in it. Communication should be done face-to-face, in-person and daily (and not via email).

Weekly one-to-ones with managers gives team members the opportunity to look at whether they've made progress during the last week (51 weeks earlier than in some firms I have worked in!).

If someone has made progress during a week, make sure you celebrate. More importantly, at the end of every 90-day cycle, make sure you celebrate. This will give your team members a sense of positive achievement and the feeling that what they've done has made a difference.

At every company I've run, we've had a celebration rhythm of an all-hands meeting every month. Total transparency was important – we shared financial information and asked each of the managers to say three positive things. They were briefed to catch people doing the right thing and call this out, awarding bottles of champagne to members from other teams who'd been particularly helpful. This behaviour always linked back to one of our core values. We also asked individuals to share the praise they'd written about teammates for the employee of the month award. Doing this in person, in public has much more impact.

The monthly all-hands was combined with a weekly email from the CEO, again putting a positive spin on what had happened that week and what was being planned for the following week. By using a regular, 'carrot not stick' rhythm, we modelled the sort of behaviour we wanted to see in the organisation and taught team members to understand what was expected of them and where the social currency was to be earned.

Encourage your teams to adopt their own personal rhythm for effective working. I'm a big fan of time-blocking – planning out your day in advance and dedicating specific hours to accomplish specific tasks. For some roles such as account management, it's important to introduce a regular rhythm around email, only checking it at certain times (ideally not before noon). This will mean they're not constantly at everyone's beck and call.

Then there's the Pomodoro Technique – another great rhythm where individuals work in regular, intensely focused bursts for 25 minutes and then give themselves a short break. I've seen first-hand how productive this can be. At Peer 1, we designed our office space around this idea, encouraging team members to take a complete mental break at regular intervals. They could shoot some pool, play a video game or simply make a coffee.

RHYTHM CREATES RESULTS

As with anything in life, to optimise the rhythm of your business is going to take deliberate practice by everyone in the company before it becomes second nature. I'm a keen runner. Like everything I do, it's my aim to get better at running with the same level of effort. Reading about running technique tells me that long-distance runners typically have a cadence of 180 steps per minute. They achieve this through subtle changes to their stride length, foot placement and body position. By regularly practising and fine-tuning my technique, I've increased the distance I can cover in the same amount of time and I feel less exhausted!

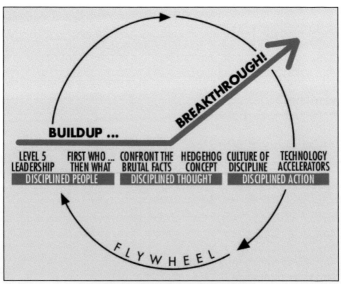

Image 6: The Flywheel Model
Source: Good To Great Jim Collins

You need to make sure that everyone in your company understands why working rhythms are important. Success will depend on total buy-in. The whole company needs to practice their working rhythms together otherwise inertia and negativity easily set in. Jim Collins uses the imagery of a flywheel. I love that. In his book, 'Good to Great' he says that no matter how dramatic the end result, good-to-great transformations never happen in one fell swoop. Rather, the process resembles relentlessly pushing a giant, heavy flywheel until it eventually builds momentum to spin on its own. As a leader, you need to spin the flywheel at the start. You have to go in every day and put the effort in. Then eventually, one day, you'll go in and find it's spinning without you – you've got to a point where your rhythm is embedded. It's become normal.

Your aim is to run a business with a higher cadence. Just like long-distance running, you want to hit that magic 180 steps per minute. Think about what you're not going to do as well as what you are. Identify ways to get more out of what you already have. Try to reduce any organisational drag that might be preventing this. Make a plan and work at it every day.

If you're deliberate from the outset, you can create new rhythms that will make a massive difference to the day-to-day functioning of your business. Introduce them as early as you can and they'll keep the momentum going as you start to grow. They'll also optimise business efficiency, working like compound interest for your company that ensures an unparalleled growth trajectory.

9. STRUCTURE

The way you structure your business can have a profound impact on customer experience. If you're a smaller business, you'll naturally be more agile. However, if you're scaling up, how do you maintain this agility?

I have faced this challenge several times. Now I am convinced in the power of structuring as a matrix organisation, with multi-disciplinary pods/stripes focusing on specific customer cohorts. These teams had daily huddles where they discussed what was happening today or tomorrow for their customers. They were bonused on the growth of their customer base and had a real sense of purpose. It was easy for them to see how their contribution made a real difference to their customers.

In my mind, this type of structure is so much more powerful than traditional models of departmental silos. It's easy to measure and point to examples of best practice that can be shared. It gives opportunities for individual growth and management training. And it means you can become huge but still deliver amazing customer service.

Structuring teams around customers is fundamental. At Rackspace, we were scaling really fast with our purpose of 'Fanatical Support'. At that time, I read a brilliant book by some Harvard Business School experts called *'Service Profit Chain: How Leading Companies Link Profit and Growth to Loyalty, Satisfaction and Value'*. It described how customer value is destroyed at the boundaries between different organisational departments. Every time a customer is forced to cross a boundary, it wrecks service. I realised this was what was happening in our competitors – the reason they were so cr*p at service was a structural thing.

We had already introduced Net Promoter Score as our metric to measure customer satisfaction and we needed a structure that maximised this. As a result, we became a matrix organisation with multi-disciplinary 'pods' focusing on specific customers. Each team had a Level 3 Windows or Linux engineer depending on the customers' operating systems, meaning customers had expert support whenever they needed it. Also in the team was a dedicated account manager along with ops and salespeople. The teams had daily huddles where they discussed what was happening today or tomorrow for each of their customers.

Remember, anything that's broken or needs fixing within your customer service offering is already known to your company. Your front-line team members will have that knowledge. Align them with customers and enable them to work with mastery, autonomy and purpose. These are the great motivators. Delivering great outcomes to customers will give their work meaning.

At Rackspace, our teams were bonused on the growth of their customer base and had a real sense of purpose. Account Managers were allowed to give up to two times the customer's monthly recurring revenue as good will credits when things went wrong. Because it was their team's money, they ended up giving away less than when they'd needed manager approval to give credits. We introduced this after a visit to Ritz Carlton and hearing about their scheme allowing employees to spend up to $2,000 to own and fix a problem. Read more about this in the fabulous Excellence Wins by founder and COO of Ritz Carlton Holtz Schulze.

Every week, we had a 'cut the cr*p' meeting where we looked at credits and examined root causes and fixes. Also feeding into this was our NPS giving recent customer comments. Combining the two created a balanced cadence of work that never got stressful.

Customers were relaxed – they knew that we knew. Their issue was on the list and we'd tell them when it was fixed. And it was easy for the team to see how their contribution made a real difference to their customers.

10. ENVIRONMENT

Lastly, but definitely not least, is your office environment. First impressions count, right? Everyone knows that. It's almost a cliché. There are various stats out there saying that judgements are formed in a matter of seconds – seven to be precise. Whether it's a new client visiting your offices for the first time or a high calibre candidate arriving for a job interview, you'll want to make sure they see the best your company can offer.

Environment is often overlooked but has a massive effect on people's motivation and performance. A cluttered, messy workplace tells me the team has a complete lack of pride in their work. Get the whole team involved in this. Talk to them about what the whole team can do to make a difference. Think about perks you can offer to make people want to come to work.

Time and again, I visit offices and discover some real horror stories. Disinterested receptionists, scruffy furniture, foul coffee... and that's if I can find the offices in the first place. This stuff is important because it says all that needs to be said about your business. If you're truly looking to grow your company, you'll need to invest time and energy into getting these details right. Because if you don't care about first impressions, your visitors will think that you don't care about anything.

Design your office space around what your team needs. Recognise that people are most effective when they work in 25-minute bursts with regular short breaks and give them things to do that provide a mental break. At Peer 1 we had pool tables exactly for this purpose. Design in a quiet space where people can concentrate and provide decent coffee that people want to drink!

Bad first impressions can be made as soon as people visit your website and can't find even the most basic of information. Directions, postcode and a phone number – it's not a lot to ask! But sometimes designers get so carried away, building aesthetically beautiful websites that bury essential information. As you search through complicated page structures, you're left thinking, 'Well, they obviously don't want to talk to me!'

Phone numbers should be visible on every page of your site and directions should be clear and easy to follow. Make sure that your postcode works in Sat Navs and Google maps. I went to see a new client recently and the address given on Google took me to his old office and not his new one. I ended up 20 minutes late for the meeting. Very frustrating!

Ditch the automated phone systems! As a business coach, I see the things that smaller businesses do thinking it makes them look bigger (but actually makes them look sh*tter). This is one of them. Just because you've installed a cloud-based PABX and it offers automated answering doesn't mean you should turn it on!

How different it is to have your call answered in 3 or 4 rings by a human being. Even better if that human being is qualified to answer your query without having to take your details and get someone else to phone back. When I took over customer experience at Peer 1, our telephone answering was automated. It took six months of battles but, eventually, I got rid of it. Team members told me it was going to cause them more work. I said they needed to shift their mindset to the awful experience our customers were getting. Hold times and abandonment rates were sky high. Sometimes customers were queuing for 3 minutes or more. It had to stop!

In our daily huddles, I told the shift managers they needed to ring every person who'd hung up in frustration the previous day and apologise that they hadn't got through. You can imagine how that went down! Within three months, the on-hold time dropped from an average of 2.5 minutes to 17 seconds. Our goal was to answer every call within three rings and have zero abandonments. It's amazing what you can achieve with daily focus.

Another pet peeve of mine is automated responses. Often, I'll find companies have an SLA around response times to tech support tickets, so they automate them. This does nothing for the customer – it's just not what people want. Automating a message to say you've received their query and will get back to them doesn't mean that they are any further forward. And it's even worse if you don't get back to them within the timeframe you've promised.

It's like those messages you get from distribution companies to say they've tried to deliver your parcel, but no-one was home. Often this is a lie. I've been working with a clear view of my driveway all day with not a van in sight. So, they've sent me an automated lie. Great! Then I go to their website and end up communicating with a chatbot. If I ask to talk to a human being, I'm told the system won't allow it.

It's so infuriating when you eventually speak to someone, only to find that they don't know who you are and can't help you. Companies often treat service as a cost and calls are answered by low-paid team members with cr*p tools.

This is one of the many things we did differently at Rackspace. Our purpose was 'Fanatical Support' and one of the ways we committed to this was ensuring all customer service calls were answered by Level 3 engineers. They knew how to fix your problem and, better still, they loved doing it. And they weren't working to the SLA, providing only acceptable levels of service.

There are times when I'm talking to someone on the phone and I can tell they don't want to help. They really should get another job! Customer service isn't in their DNA. I remember a while back, when I was working at Pipex, a distraught customer called me on a Saturday. She'd been through a huge ordeal, caring for her dying father who'd been diagnosed with lung cancer. During this time, we hadn't been able to reach her as her server had been hacked and she didn't have a separate email address. Now our solicitors were after her for an unpaid debt of £1,000.

I spent half an hour reassuring her and told her that I'd write off the debt. In the office the following Monday, I spoke to our Customer Service Manager to arrange this. Do you know what she said? 'How do you know that story's true – did her father really die?' I was staggered. I suspected that attitude had served her well in the past but it didn't work for me.

In contrast, I had a fantastic experience when I visited the offices of WebMart. The founder's PA, Lisa, rang me the day before, making sure I had the right directions and asking me for my hot beverage of choice, so they could get it ready for my arrival. She told me where I should park and to follow the red carpet up to the door – talk about celebrity treatment! I was then met by a charming young lady whose enthusiasm for the company was infectious. She gave me a tour of the building and, by the time I arrived at the meeting, I could tell I was in a purpose-driven business with engaged, happy team members.

Sounds obvious but your Reception area is where first impressions are formed. As the story I've just described at WebMart shows, you can pick up the buzz of a place just from the welcome you receive when you walk through the door. It's like entering a hive. In successful companies, someone will come and ask you quickly if you are ok, offer you a hot drink and deal with you efficiently and quickly. There are places I've been (particularly in London where Reception is outsourced) where no-one makes eye contact as you check-in and you're abandoned to sit on shabby furniture, leafing through coffee-stained magazines.

Your Reception area needs to reflect your business. It's a golden opportunity to impress and you can communicate so many messages through it. The reception, and the whole office should be tidy. How could I expect team members to care about the customer experience if they didn't care about their own surroundings? By improving our environment, we raise the bar for excellence. I want everyone to feel, from the moment they walked in, that we had high expectations of them. And I did this by providing a workplace that they were proud of.

It's amazing the difference you can have by making a bit of an effort for a visitor. Great coffee is a must but after I'd experienced a welcome tray at ?WHATIF!, a business innovation company, we started serving homemade cake. This arrived every time a client came to us for a meeting. It created a sense of theatre around the sales process. It instantly said, 'We've made an effort' and gave prospective clients a sense of the service they could expect. Our quote conversion rate rose from 40% when we visited clients to 80% when they came to us and were given Sam's mum's cake!

And finally, don't forget about the toilet. Your washroom facilities are a window into your company's soul. If you can eat off the floor of the toilets in a restaurant, then you don't need to worry about their kitchen cleanliness. Again, it comes back to making an effort and attention to detail. The only hand-dryers that work are Dyson Airblades, so make sure you have them. If your Finance Director tells you they're too expensive, argue that you're changing the mindset of your business to drive towards excellence in everything that you do.

At Peer 1, our loo was twinned with another in Africa – a really worthwhile project that had been the suggestion of a team member. Another positive message. Even your toilets can tell a story.

I recently went to see a potential new client and knew, as soon as I walked through the door, that I wasn't a good fit for their business. The doormat was worn, the stairwell smelled like a public toilet and his Receptionist ignored me when I arrived. This client was in love with the idea of coaching but I could tell he didn't want to make the effort needed to succeed.

Improving the office environment requires investing money and making change a priority, but one that pays off. It is part of the obsessive attention to detail and a real drive to succeed that scaling up a business requires.

PART 4

BRINGING IT ALL TOGETHER

BRINGING IT ALL TOGETHER

* —

The ideas, methods and core principles discussed in parts 2 and 3 of this book are all things that I have personally used to improve employee wellbeing, scale up and grow businesses. The task is not easy, and the 10 point plan takes time, but if you are consistent with implementing the steps and you have a real drive to succeed then you will see improvements, growth and revenue.

However, before I let you go away and do the work, I want to make sure you are clear on the tools I've discussed in this book, and offer a few more tools that you can use on your road to success.

ONE PAGE PERSONAL PLAN

The One Page Personal Plan (OPPP) is about getting people to dig deep, find out what they really want, to write it down and share it. Most people don't ever do that but planning and sharing can help us focus and give us purpose.

Where do you see yourself in 10 to 25 years' time? That's a big question, isn't it? Have you ever actually thought about what you REALLY want from life? A lot of people haven't. It seems so far off. But thinking about that end goal can actually help you focus on the here and now.

A handy exercise I like to use with clients is the One Page Personal Plan (OPPP). I find it useful because it helps people formulate an image of where they want to get to in their lives, as a precursor to establishing where they want their business to be too. I ask clients to take part in these exercises first because many of us launch companies for a reason. That reason is usually linked to our personal motivations and our personal purpose in life. Often, I find people haven't thought about it explicitly; we get caught up in everyday life, the churn of day to day business. But if we think about where we want to be explicitly from a personal perspective *before* we think about it from a business perspective, it enables me to help clients create the right context for thinking about the business.

At the top of the OPPP, there is a space for the date. Pick a date that's between 10 and 25 years in the future. Perhaps your birthday, an anniversary, something you're going to remember, a date that has meaning for you. Then go through each of the sections thinking about what you want those things to be like on that specific date.

- RELATIONSHIPS – Who would you like to have in your life? Your children? Your husband/wife? Perhaps you want to be married by then? Put all this down.

- ACHIEVEMENTS – Do you want to have run 5 marathons? Climbed Mount Kilimanjaro? Written a book? Set up a charity? What is it you would like to have accomplished?

- RITUALS – What are the rituals that are going to be an important part of your life? The things you do on a regular basis. It might be going to church. It could be sailing, playing golf, doing more yoga, cooking. Anything you would like to be doing often.

- WEALTH – This might not necessarily be money, perhaps it's time. But if it is money you need to get specific. How much? What's your current cost of living? How much do you need to have saved by then? If it is more time you want, you might want to say that by this date you'll have built your business in a way that allows you to run it one day a week, not five.

NAME _____   DATE _____

		RELATIONSHIPS	ACHIEVEMENTS	RITUALS	WEALTH (£)
FAITH	10-25 YEARS (ASPIRATIONS)				
FAMILY	1 YEAR (ACTIVITIES)				
FRIENDS		START	START	START	START
FITNESS	90 DAYS (ACTIONS)				
		STOP	STOP	STOP	STOP
FINANCE					

Image 7: One Page Personal Plan (OPPP)
Source: Scaling Up Verne Harnish

If you look down the right side of the page you'll notice five words there – Finance, Fitness, Friends, Family and Faith. These are all things that successful people have said they were able to take care of that meant they felt content. So, when you're writing your list think about how they fit into those categories. And faith doesn't have to mean religion, it could mean spirituality. Whatever fits you best.

Everything that's written down needs to be very specific. Cameron Herold in his book *'Double Double'* said he wanted his company to be a Harvard Business Review case study and they wrote it down, they put it on the wall, and it became a reality. It's not a personal achievement exactly, but it's the same. Jeff Hoffman in the book *'Scale'* said he wanted to travel to 50 different countries and once he made that explicit he ended up setting up a travel company and achieving it. It's another mental trick. If you just say you want to travel it probably won't happen, but, if you say I want to go travelling and I want to go to South America for three months in the next 3 years, then it is more likely to happen because you're being much more specific. These are all things we have control over. Just like business. If we want it to happen in this very specific way, we'll work out a way of doing it.

Once you've completed the 10 to 25 years section of the plan it's time to work it back to 12 months from now. Go through the sections again, what would you need to be doing in a year from now to be on a trajectory through that 12 months out to the 10 – 25 years goal?

Then it's time to think about the next 90 days. You need to work out what you need to do in the next 90 days that'll help you hit those targets at 12 months, and then on to 10/25 years. The Stop/Start lists are really helpful, again, to be very specific. What do you need to start doing straight away to meet those targets? Start going to yoga once a week. Save £500 a month. Visit Mum. Review your pension plan with a financial advisor. In my case, it's taking my daughter each week to the local climbing wall that she loves.

This is a personal call to action. You now know what your plan is. Where you want to be and how you're going to get there. Follow it up every 90 days with where you've got to. You might find your 12 month goal needs moving out by a quarter, but that's fine because you still know where you are and where you want to be. Go back and make another set of actions to complete over the coming 90 days.

HOW TO IDENTIFY DYSFUNCTIONAL TEAM BEHAVIOURS

Once you've done the One Page Personal Plan (OPPP) of where you personally want to go in life, the next step is to look at your business and your team.

We've all seen dysfunctional teams in the workplace, and most of us will have been part of one at some point in our careers. They can have a negative impact both personally and professionally.

When I was working at Peer1 it was obvious there was dysfunction within some of the team, so I asked a leadership coach to run a session with the leadership team and the sales team combined. I wanted to address performance issues and also flesh out the cause of the dysfunction. I was so impressed by the outcome of Nikki's session that I use the exercise with my own clients today. It works.

First, let's begin the meeting (and this can be incorporated into all meetings) with some deep sharing. Google identified this as a way of building psychological safety, which is essential in driving team performance and allows people to say what they really need to say.

What I tend to do with clients is get them to tell me where they were born, how many siblings they have, where in the order they come, and what the biggest challenge was that they overcame as a child by age 12. Pick someone to start who you know will share something really personal because then it sets the tone and everybody else will feel compelled to go to the same level. If I am running this session with a CEO and their team I start with them.

Once that is out the way we can move onto the saboteur exercise, which I've now done with many clients and teams in my own organisations. What's the point? Well, we know this team has some behaviours which are self-destructive or counter-productive. Maybe it's gossip, maybe backbiting, it could be a lack of support for one another, whatever it is there's something about this team that's led to them forming a pattern of behaviour that is stopping them being as good as they could be. The sum of the parts is less than the whole. This exercise will shine a spotlight on the behaviours that are holding them back. Then I want the team to realise that these behaviours might be counterproductive and agree themselves that they should change them.

So, the first thing to ask is — "who do you hate?" Here I want them to give me their competitor. It's interesting because sometimes even this can throw up issues. I often find organisations don't know who their competitor is and that means they don't have a really clear position in the market. Food for thought even before the real exercise begins!

Sometimes it's easy to pick a competitor and sometimes it isn't, but we settle on somebody that we hate. Oh, I know at this point some of you are complaining that hate is such a negative word. Use whatever word sums up strong negative emotion. When I think hate I am thinking Newcastle vs Sunderland, Liverpool vs Man Utd or Man United and everyone else. Next I get them to imagine this competitor has hired them to stay within their current job and sabotage the company from within. It is their job to undermine their current employer in lots of small ways.

In small groups, they get a pen and a flip chart so they can brainstorm all the ways in which they would sabotage the company. Everything. The answers often include:
- Make promises we don't keep
- Sell things below cost
- Lie to clients
- Ship faulty products
- Hire terrible people
- Promote the wrong people
- Steal things to make the company less profitable... and so on....

People have no problem coming up with these ideas, they fill their flip chart in minutes. What I love about this exercise is how much fun it is for those taking part, how excited they get. These are grown-ups that get so excited in a way that somehow they don't seem to get so excited about some of the other exercises I get people to do! There's always high energy in the room and lots of activity and engagement. It's fun, but there's a really powerful outcome to it.

Once they've finished all their ideas they put them on the wall and tick all the behaviours they've seen in their own team. Some of them might get ticked, all of them might get ticked. Then they get this realisation that they don't actually need their competitor to hire saboteurs to work in the business, in fact they don't need the competition at all because they are quite capable of destroying their own business from the inside out in a mindless way. It's a big "wow" moment when they say, "look at what we're doing to ourselves."

So, I ask—"What should we do?" Somebody will always say they should stop doing some of these things and of course everybody agrees because that seems to be the completely normal rational thing to do!

We then go through each behaviour, turning it from a negative into a positive that can become part of a team charter or manifesto. We want around ten rules that this team is now going to live by. And because it's their words they are more able to hold each other accountable to their new behavioural standards.

They could include—make a promise, keep a promise. Practice radical candour. They might bring in a new recruitment plan, or set a rule to give one-on-one feedback every week. There might be something about supporting other employees to be successful. This is all about creating a list of positive things because in any team there will be a spectrum of skills, ability and attitude and we want to get everyone on the same page, heading in the same direction. To turn the team around. Every game has rules and white lines. This allows the team to write the rules of the new game and they clearly agree on the white lines and out of bounds.

"Teamwork is the ability to work together toward a common vision. The ability to direct individual accomplishments toward organisational objectives. It is the fuel that allows common people to attain uncommon results." - Andrew Carnegie

What happens going forward is that people will make sure everyone on the team sticks to the charter, and if they don't they'll call them out for that. They'll feel that the team can be as successful as it can be if they live by their new team rules. I've had people say that it's changed their lives as well as the team. Certainly, at Peer1 when we took part in the exercise, we did then lose a couple of team members, so very quickly we went from having a dysfunctional team to having a cohesive team on the mend.

GROWING YOUR BUSINESS THROUGH EMPLOYEE ENGAGEMENT

I love the Gallup Q12! It's a fantastic metric of 12 questions in a pyramid that measure the most important elements of employee engagement. Wherever I've been MD, I've used it. It has helped me scale two UK companies from zero revenue to £30 million in just five years.

If you're looking to grow your company, you need to know where you're at and where you're heading. How can you do that without regular, systematic measurement? As a Business Coach, I speak at events and it amazes me that the majority of CEOs in the room have no handle on employee engagement. That's crazy! Numerous studies have shown a direct link between high levels of engagement and business results. Engaged team members believe in the purpose of the firm and give you up to 40% of additional effort.

At a macro level, Gallup is saying that 87% of the UK workforce is not engaged. That's phenomenal. Most people are going through their working life on autopilot. What a waste of an existence! I feel so passionately about this. The kick I get out of coaching is I can see how much faster everything happens when you have an engaged workforce. And it's much more fun – for me and my clients!

The aim of the Gallup survey is to identify the 12 elements of good management. Gallup can run it for you, or you can manage it yourself. It tells you where you need to focus your effort and it's invaluable for building high-performing teams and positive, productive working environments. So, what are the 12 questions?

Q1 – DO YOU KNOW WHAT'S EXPECTED OF YOU AT WORK?

A simple question but wow, can this tell you a lot. Gallup's benchmarks require you to get 75% of all team members giving this 5/5 to be in their top quartile of firms they study. And if you don't? You need to bring in OKRs to give your teams quantitative clarity on what a good day is and what to measure. You want your whole team to get to the end of their day and know they've done well.

Time and again I see the power of this. Whether it's hours on the phone for sales people or time recorded against tickets for engineers on the Support Desk, ensure all team members have real-time information on how well they're doing. They need to know what a good day looks like. It's so motivating. This can change behaviours overnight. People who do a good job are recognised. Those who don't have to either step up or get out.

If you don't have them already, also introduce daily huddles for the whole team where everyone discusses their commitments for the day. Doing this in public is powerful. It gives greater accountability and responsibility. We see this in our lives outside work. It's easier to train or lose weight with an accountability partner.

Q2 – DO YOU HAVE THE MATERIALS AND EQUIPMENT YOU NEED TO DO YOUR WORK RIGHT?

How many times have I been in offices where people are surrounded by broken stuff and dodgy ways of doing things? It's amazing the levels of complacency I've seen. You can build a whole system around this question. When I've been a judge in awards programmes, I've sensed this from my experience of a firm's reception area; broken lights, wobbly chairs, out of date press clippings and pervasive lack of care.

Q3 – AT WORK, DO YOU HAVE THE OPPORTUNITY TO DO WHAT YOU DO BEST EVERY DAY?

This is where another tool comes in handy – the Gallup StrengthsFinder. It doesn't concentrate on things people are good at, but rather the things that give them energy. Activities that motivate and give them joy. This can help you get the right people on the bus, in the right seats. Whatever the job is, there's likely to be someone in your organisation for whom it's a strength. If you give work to people who enjoy it, it gets done better.

Your managers need to be aware of this. One way is to get team members to keep diaries. Over the space of a few months, ask them to set their phones to bleep every 15 minutes or so. Get them to write down whether they're enjoying what they're doing. You'll see their loves and their loathes. In the team, there should be enough difference between team members to share these out. If not, then put together the collective loathes and hire someone who loves to do this stuff. Now, you'll have a high performing team!

Q4 – IN THE LAST 7 DAYS, HAVE YOU RECEIVED RECOGNITION OR PRAISE FOR DOING GOOD WORK?

In the past, some managers have told me they worry that if they praise too often it will lose its impact. Nonsense! I have never worked in or visited a firm where team members complained of being over-praised. I guess if that happens, you could recalibrate but, until then, you aren't doing it enough – by a long way.

This question can tell you so much about your managers. Praise and recognition are fundamental to happiness at work and you want to foster a culture of celebration. 7 days is deliberate – it's very recent. Team members should instantly recall a moment where their contribution was recognised.

To be in the top quartile nationally, you need more than half of everyone in your team to rate this 5/5. I recommend you have an all-hands meeting every month where you share financial information and ask each of the managers to say three positive things. Ensure they're briefed to catch people doing the right thing and call this out, giving awards wherever possible. Recognition and praise need to become an automatic part of the rhythm of your business.

Q5 – DOES YOUR SUPERVISOR SEEM TO CARE ABOUT YOU AS A PERSON?

Man! Bring humanity into work! We spend a third of our lives working. If individuals think nobody cares about them at work, that's heart-breaking. We've all worked in toxic environments where it's not the norm and it makes for a miserable existence. Again, this question will tell you a lot about your managers. It's their responsibility to ensure all team members feel valued and listened to.

Q6 – IS THERE SOMEONE AT WORK WHO ENCOURAGES YOUR DEVELOPMENT?

Your managers should be coaches. If you get a low score on this question, it will tell you where you need to focus. As well as looking at management, you could also roll out a peer coaching programme – these can turn things around quickly. It costs nothing and doesn't need specific rules or training. Every team member can pick someone as their coach, agreeing how often to meet. This can be fabulous for an organisation.

Q7 – AT WORK DO YOUR OPINIONS SEEM TO COUNT?

You really want everyone in your team to be saying yes to this one. It comes back to daily huddles and weekly meetings with the team. Regular opportunities to talk to a manager about daily blocks and challenges. If team members have opinions on something, they need to feel like they're being heard.

As mentioned earlier, when I'm coaching leadership teams, I tell them to talk to at least one person outside of their team every week as well as a customer. It means every time you get together to discuss progress in the business, you'll be able to share six conversations with team members and six with customers – a much more informed leadership meeting! If an incident happens, you'll have a pulse on team members and customer impact. It's impossible to think that individuals wouldn't feel heard in this situation as a six person SLT will have had over 300 conversations with team members outside of their teams in a year.

Q8 – DOES THE MISSION/PURPOSE OF YOUR COMPANY MAKE YOU FEEL YOUR JOB IS IMPORTANT?

Well, if it doesn't, you've done a cr*p job of defining your purpose! It's a fact that now, more than ever, people are yearning for a higher sense of purpose – of shared values and meaning in their working existence. They want to make their lives count for something. So, as CEO, you need to be thinking 'How do we create a great place to work?' Part of that is saying, 'How do we make work meaningful?' and 'What is our purpose?'

This question is a great sanity check for management. It's a good test to see if your company's purpose still resonates. I recently worked with a CEO who was clear about his company's purpose and what it stood for. But his leadership team had lost sight of it. You could guarantee that if they didn't know it, then there was no hope for the rest of his team. We didn't need to change the purpose itself but we worked on communicating it better.

Q9 – ARE YOUR FELLOW EMPLOYEES COMMITTED TO DOING QUALITY WORK?

'A Players' hate working with 'B' and 'C Players' – fact! This question will tell you if there's a problem with performance. The beauty of the Gallup survey is you'll get a sense of this team by team, manager by manager. You'll know which teams aren't committed to quality. There's nothing more demotivating than feeling you're working harder or better than someone else but getting paid the same, or less.

This question will give you the data to take action. Introduce OKRs so that everyone knows what's expected and root out poor performers. If you don't, your business will be mired in mediocrity.

Q10 – DO YOU HAVE A BEST FRIEND AT WORK?

This is one of the most intriguing questions in the Q12! It's based on research showing a concrete link between having a best friend in the workplace and high performing teams. This can cause some hilarity when you roll it out. But it makes sense. If team members feel there's someone they can turn to, who has their back, they're more likely to feel secure and happy.

I often wonder whether Gallup has looked into whether remote working versus office working makes a difference to this. To my mind, there's no substitute for face-to-face. In the past, people have stayed longer than they needed to in my teams because they were genuine friends. It's so worth the effort. Encourage your team to spend time with each other, both in and out of the office. It will pay dividends for productivity. I'm also a big fan of moving team members around different desks and departments to widen social networks.

Q11 – IN THE LAST SIX MONTHS, HAS SOMEONE AT WORK TALKED TO YOU ABOUT YOUR PROGRESS?

This is all about the rhythms in your company. Annual appraisal systems are not worth the effort and aggro they create. Bin them! Instead, introduce a daily, weekly, monthly and quarterly rhythm that gives regular opportunities for open and honest feedback. Do this, and you should be able to get 100% of your company saying yes to this question. To be in the top quartile, it only needs to be above 60%.

Q12 – IN THE LAST YEAR, HAVE YOU HAD OPPORTUNITIES TO LEARN AND GROW?

This final question will speak volumes about your managers. Your managers should be coaches. Instead of directing people, they should be motivating, supporting, encouraging and rewarding in every one of their interactions. This unlocks potential in teams like nothing else, increasing engagement and productivity. My view is that someone shouldn't be promoted to management unless they can show they're up to being an effective coach. It's a fundamental part of their role.

By the end of the Gallup Q12 process, you'll have a score for every one of your managers. If you've got an employee retention issue, you can bet it's driven by poor management and this will enable you to root it out. You'll also get to see where the pockets of best practice exist in your organisation. Find these and you can share them. Learning from each other is a key part of scaling up.

MAKE SURE YOUR CUSTOMERS ARE HAPPY

I went into great detail in the part 2 section, 'Your customer is king', but it is worth reiterating the importance of the Net Promoter Score. It's always puzzled me why so many businesses focus on finding new customers rather than keeping the ones they've got? Research shows that it costs five times more to do this. And this is even more crazy as existing customers are 50% more likely to try new products compared to new customers. Increasing customer retention rates by 5% increases profits by anything between 25 and 95%. That's staggering!

Fred Reichheld spent two years refining a single, all-important question that linked actual customer behaviour (purchasing patterns and referrals) with company growth: **'Would you recommend (name of company) to a friend or colleague?'**

A regular feedback mechanism like NPS will give your team members real-time information on how they're doing. It's a brilliant motivator. At the end of last year, I interviewed Tony Pandher, Head of Ops at Macquarie Cloud Services for an episode of The Melting Pot with Dominic Monkhouse. He's 'gamified' NPS by creating 'The League of Legends'. If their support technicians get 10 x 10s in a row on their NPS transaction tickets, they take part in this prestigious, monthly competition. They are the heroes of the organisation.

Sales is all about confidence. And what better way to build confidence than by getting salespeople to talk to happy customers. I suggest that your new business sales team calls all customers who've scored you as a 9 or 10. If they're fed with these positive news stories, they will be more confident in their marketplace.

As a Business Coach, I meet people who are negative about NPS. They tell me they tried it and it didn't work. When I delve a bit deeper, I'm struck that it's like learning to swim by reading a book. They've rolled it out with a really shallow understanding of what it takes to make it a success. There are some fantastic resources available telling you everything you need to know but using it successfully takes deliberate practice and effort. It doesn't come easily.

SALES VELOCITY

'I don't have enough leads'. Sound familiar? How often do you hear this excuse from your salespeople? It's pretty common for sales strategies to fixate on the number of opportunities won or lost.

But what if I told you that your team could do 30% better than they are today with their existing pipeline? How? By focusing on the four elements of the sales velocity equation.

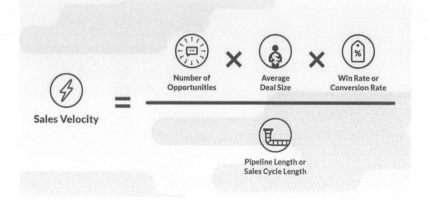

Image 8: Sales Velocity Equation

Put simply, sales velocity is a measurement of how fast you're making money. It shows how quickly leads are moving through your pipeline and how much value new customers provide over a certain time period. The less time it takes for prospects to progress, the faster you can close more deals. So, a higher sales velocity means your salespeople are bringing in more revenue in less time.

Measuring and improving these elements of your sales cycle will have a massive effect on your business. An increase of 10% in deal value and win rate and a reduction of 10% in sales cycle length, will increase your sales velocity by 34%. Without any change in the number of sales opportunities. A dramatic uplift in revenue!

But it's not just the velocity that matters - another fast way to increase revenue is increasing a deals value.

It's important to track the average order value and level of discounting going on within your sales team. It's all too easy to end up with margin leakage.

You need this data for each and every sales rep — their average deal size and average margin per month. Quite often I request this information from clients and people just don't know. They're unaware of what the product or services profitability is. They don't know what the deal should have been sold at before the discount and also what the discount was. Make sure your CRM is set up to track this so that when you're doing your pricing, you record both the list price and the actual price the salesperson gets for it.

As well as looking at price and discounts, you need to think of how you're bundling your offering. What are you making it easy for customers to buy? Are you maximising every customer interaction with your business?

McDonald's is a great example of this concept at work. Instead of focusing on footfall, they decided to maximise the margin from every interaction. So whenever you order a meal, you're given the option to 'go large for 50p'. Simple but oh so effective. Supermarket meal deals are another one — instead of just buying a sandwich, you walk out of the shop with a drink, crisps, snack etc.

Ask yourself, 'What is the thing that looks like incredible value to my customer but is low cost to my business?' In the hosting world, we threw in discounted firewalls or free security products. The client would perceive these to be high value but, because they were automated services, they were low cost to us. So, if you sell A to a customer then could you also sell B, C and D with A? So many times, either companies or individual sales reps aren't good at thinking in this way — either there's no programme or it's inconsistently delivered.

One other thing on deal values. Where they're static, it's often because there's no ownership of key areas of the business. You need separate accountabilities for Sales, Product Management and New Product Development. Quite often, where organisations are selling someone else's product (e.g. Microsoft or Dell resellers), there's no service definition and nobody is looking to improve services or put up the price to drive margin. And someone needs to own deal values – if deal values aren't increasing, it's because there's no one in that seat.

We live in a world that's increasingly driven by monthly recurring revenue (MRR). Instead of focusing on product sales or one-off projects, businesses are looking at selling pre and post services with annuity revenue. If you're Chief Executive of a Managed Services Provider (MSP), your aim should be to get this up to at least 50% of your business. Only then will you pass the tipping point, getting your company into higher multiples in terms of valuation.

At all three of the MSPs where I've been MD (Rackspace, Peer 1 and IT Lab), our business was driven by recurring revenue. We were obsessed with it. Every day, we worked out our net sales position in terms of monthly recurring revenue. And we did what we could to drive it up every day, month, quarter and year.

I recently worked with a guy whose business sold hardware – printers mainly. We looked at how to turn product revenue into services revenue. My advice was to offer a pre-service, the product itself and then post service. As we discussed this in more depth, he suddenly leaned over and hit his head on the desk. You could call it his Damascus moment. 'Oh God,' he said. 'Now I get it. I went in to see a client last week and did a printer audit for them, for free. I should have charged for it!' It turned out that he'd told this client that if they bought new printers from him, it could lead to annual savings of £200K. 'And…?' I prompted. He continued, 'And if I'd sold them a managed services contract for £150K, I could have given away the printers for free. I'd still have saved them £50K a year but would have walked away with £150K of recurring revenue!' Perfect. Moments like that are priceless when you're a coach!

In my experience, sales managers are successful when they're clear about their expectations and share sales velocity data in real-time. If you want your reps to be selling at the right price (not discounting) and bundling properly, you need complete clarity over what you want people to do. And they need to be shown information that proves other reps are managing to achieve this.

Every week, look at who's doing best/worst for discounts and hence margin. What are they doing differently to the others? How do you get the others to look more like the best? Humans are inherently tribal animals. We like to follow the herd. By taking this approach, you'll encourage weaker members of the sales team to up their game to be more like the others. And if they don't? You need to replace them.

When you go out to hire, make sure that as part of your interview process, you test the understanding of the difference between price and margin. Often sales people are rubbish at this. But it's symptomatic of a wider issue that companies are generally poor at managing margin.

Most of the time, organisations measure the number of opportunities worked by the sales person. This is because the sales team isn't hitting its target. Before too long, it descends into a blame game. 'It's Marketing's fault. They're not giving us enough leads etc'.

When this is the case, my observation is that the true fault lies with a lack of definition of core customer. And consequently, sales people have no unique proposition to take to market. You need to be clear about who you serve, the problem you fix and how you do it better than anyone else. It's so, so important. Without this, it will be impossible to build a machine to drive opportunity volume.

Your close rate for sales should be running at around 50%. Otherwise, you're over proposing. I worked with a client last year whose win rate was 10% – it was clear we had work to do! Quite quickly, I pinpointed what was happening in their sales cycle. It came down to a lack of deals in the pipeline. His sales team were writing proposals so that they had something to talk about at the weekly ordeal of sales meetings. Everyone was under the cosh, with huge pressure on sales to do more. They looked busy but their activity wasn't resulting in more revenue. Of course, this drove down their close rate.

The average win rate in the tech sector is about 30%. But only 15% of salespeople hit their quota every year, telling you that most of them are poor at what they do. So, if you're building a team of salespeople that are above average, you should be looking for a 50% close rate out of the whole team. If they do that, they're working fewer opportunities but working them at more depth. The easiest way to do that is to define your core customer. Stop your salespeople chasing after unwinnable deals.

MEASURING THE FOUR AREAS OF SALES VELOCITY

Keeping a consistent rhythm of measurement and feedback will pay dividends with your sales team. Make sure your CRM is set up to give you data on all four areas of the sales velocity equation. Look in detail at these metrics and the value of your pipeline every week.

Be clear about your expectations of what every member of the team should be doing.

With daily feedback, salespeople can see where they rank and, if they're near the bottom, face up to the fact they need to do better. Give them their stack ranking on the number of opportunities, average deal value, win rate, length of sales cycle and their overall pipeline. Get every one of them to focus on what they can do to improve these stats. If the length of their sales cycle is too long, how do they shorten it? It's so common for salespeople to spend too long waiting for a sale or waste time chasing deals that are dead. Far better to focus on the deals they can win.

Tracking sales velocity can be invaluable to a growing business. Over time, it will allow you to benchmark against other teams, compare the effectiveness of individual reps and regions and see how changes to the sales process impact your business, for better or worse. Understanding sales velocity will also help you forecast more accurately and determine how your sale process can be optimised for faster sales and higher conversion rates. That's got to be a good thing!

CONCLUSION

As MD of Rackspace, people used to ask me, 'Dom – how would you describe the company?' My answer was always, 'Culture heavy. Process light'. We put a shed-load of effort into hiring the right people, putting them in small teams and allowing them to make decisions. Managers became coaches and we supported our front line teams to do the work that their customers thought was important.

That was at the heart of why we grew so quickly. And it's the reason why this book has been focused so heavily on culture as a mechanism for execution. Your customers won't love your company until your staff do, so concentrate on the things that will boost staff engagement and happiness levels. And when your customers start to love you, do everything in your power to keep them.

Of course, there are gaps and I will leave strategy for another day. This is not a discussion about the tools I use as a business coach. Instead, it is a retrospective gathering of all the things that helped me scale three businesses. Henry Stewart, author of 'The Happiness Manifesto', once introduced me as 'a magpie' before a presentation I was due to give. He said he'd never met anyone who was better at spotting a shiny object in another business and implementing it. My hope is that you can take these shiny objects and put them to good use in your own business.

BIBLIOGRAPHY

BOOKS

Scaling Up: How a Few Companies Make It...and Why the Rest Don't (Rockefeller Habits 2.0) - by *Verne Harnish*

The Ultimate Question 2.0 (Revised and Expanded Edition): How Net Promoter Companies Thrive in a Customer-Driven World - by *Fred Reichheld and Rob Markey*

Mastering the Rockefeller Habits: What You Must Do to Increase the Value of Your Fast-growth Firm - by *Verne Harnish*

Topgrading - by *Bradford D Smart*

Everyone Culture - by *Robert Kegan, Lisa Laskow Lahey, Matthew L Miller, Andy Fleming, Deborah Helsing*

3HAG Way: The Strategic Execution System That Ensures Your Strategy Is Not a Wild-Ass-Guess! - by *Shannon Byrne Susko*

First, Break All The Rules - by *Marcus Buckingham*

Strengthsfinder 2.0: A New and Upgraded Edition of the Online Test from Gallup's Now Discover Your Strengths - by *Tom Rath*

Good To Great - by *Jim Collins*

12: Elements of Great Managing: The Elements of Great Managing - by *Rodd Wagner*

Decide and Deliver: Five Steps to Breakthrough Performance in Your Organization - by *Marcia Blenko, Michael C. Mankins, Paul Rogers*

Excellence Wins - *by Horst Schulze*

ARTICLES

Turning Goals into Results: The Power of Catalytic Mechanisms by *Jim Collins* (Harvard Business Review, July/August 1999)

The One Number You Need to Grow - by *Frederick F. Reichheld* (Harvard Business Review, December 2003)

Elon Musk tries to avoid having meetings at Tesla — and encourages people to leave if they're not adding any value - by *Justin Bariso* (www.inc.com, March 2020)

A Portrait of the Overperforming Salesperson - by *Steve W. Martin* (Harvard Business Review, June 2016)

Printed in Great Britain
by Amazon